AMANDA OTIS

Daily Doses of Positivity

365 Days of Affirmations and Reflection Questions for Happiness, Success, and Personal Growth

OTIS

Contents

1

Introduction

Positive affirmations have long been recognized as a transformative tool for influencing one's mindset and overall well-being. These affirmations, which are concise and positive statements, have been utilized across cultures and eras to foster mental health, reshape thought patterns, and enhance success and fulfillment. Rooted in both psychology and philosophy, affirmations offer a simple yet profound way to effect change in various areas of life.

Historically, the use of affirmations can be traced back to ancient spiritual practices and philosophical teachings. Philosophers like the Stoics and various Eastern traditions believed in the power of positive self-talk to influence one's emotions and behavior. Over time, this practice evolved and became integrated into modern psychological theories, particularly those focused on cognitive restructuring and self-empowerment. In contemporary settings, affirmations have gained renewed attention for their role in personal development, largely due to their accessibility and effectiveness in a world that often feels overwhelming and fast-paced.

In today's society, where stress and busyness are common, affirmations offer a straightforward method to combat negativity and promote a healthier mental state. They work by repeatedly reinforcing positive beliefs and behaviors, which gradually shift one's internal dialogue and outlook. This practice helps to counteract the pervasive negativity and self-doubt that can arise in our daily lives, creating a more optimistic and resilient mindset.

This book explores the multifaceted benefits of positive affirmations and their application across different areas of life. It explores how affirmations can improve mental health by reducing anxiety and boosting self-esteem, offering a counterbalance to the negative thought patterns that often accompany mental health struggles. Individuals can cultivate a more positive self-image and enhance their emotional well-being by focusing on affirmations related to self-worth and personal strength.

In addition to mental health, affirmations play a significant role in achieving success and fulfillment. By regularly affirming one's goals and capabilities, individuals can foster a growth-oriented mindset that drives them toward their aspirations. Affirmations such as "I am capable of achieving my goals" or "I am open to new opportunities" help maintain focus and motivation, paving the way for success in various endeavors.

Affirmations also have a profound impact on relationships. By promoting self-love and empathy, affirmations can enhance interpersonal connections and foster more meaningful and supportive relationships. Statements like "I communicate with kindness and understanding" or "I am worthy of love and respect" help build a positive foundation for interactions with others, leading to more fulfilling and harmonious relationships.

This book is not only a comprehensive guide, but also includes 365 days of affirmations, each accompanied by reflection questions designed to deepen your engagement with the practice. These daily affirmations and reflective prompts are crafted to guide you through a year-long journey of positivity and self-discovery. By incorporating these affirmations into your daily routine, you will have the opportunity to address various aspects of your life, from personal growth and emotional resilience to success and relationship building.

The book's reflection questions are designed to help you internalize and personalize the affirmations. They encourage you to explore your thoughts, feelings, and experiences in relation to them, fostering a deeper understanding of their impact on your life. This reflective practice enhances the effectiveness of the affirmations, allowing you to align them more closely with your personal goals and values.

Positive affirmations offer a powerful and accessible method for personal development and well-being. By integrating these affirmations into your daily life, you can transform your mindset, improve your mental health, and achieve greater success and fulfillment. The combination of affirmations and reflective questions in this book provides a structured approach to harnessing the power of positive thinking, guiding you toward a more optimistic and empowered life.

As you embark on this journey, remember that the key to success with affirmations lies in consistency and belief. Regular practice and a genuine conviction in the positive statements you affirm will amplify their impact, helping you create meaningful and lasting change in your life. Embrace the practice of positive affirmations with dedication and openness, and discover the profound benefits they can bring to your mental well-being, success, and overall happiness.

2

Chapter 1: Understanding Positive Affirmations

Definition and Origins

Positive affirmations are carefully crafted, intentional statements designed to positively influence your mindset and
emotional well-being. By repeating these affirmations, you
engage in a powerful practice of self-talk that directly impacts
your thoughts, feelings, and ultimately, your actions. This
practice is rooted in the idea that the words we speak to
ourselves have the potential to shape our reality by altering
our inner dialogue and the way we perceive the world around
us.

The concept of affirmations is far from a modern invention. In
fact, it has deep historical roots that stretch back to ancient
civilizations. Among these early adopters were the Stoics,
a group of philosophers in ancient Greece and Rome who
placed immense value on the power of self-talk. The Stoics
believed that by consciously guiding their thoughts through

positive self-affirmations, they could maintain control over their emotions and responses to external events, no matter how challenging those events might be.

For the Stoics, the practice of affirmations was a means of cultivating resilience and inner peace. They understood that our thoughts are the precursors to our emotions, and by mastering the art of positive self-talk, one could effectively navigate life's ups and downs with a sense of calm and purpose. This ancient wisdom has transcended time, and today, people continue to harness the power of affirmations as a tool for personal growth, emotional balance, and mental fortitude. Whether spoken aloud or silently, positive affirmations serve as a powerful reminder of our ability to shape our thoughts and, in turn, our lives.

The Psychology Behind Affirmations

The psychological underpinnings of affirmations are deeply rooted in the principles of cognitive-behavioral therapy (CBT), a well-established therapeutic approach that focuses on the intricate relationship between our thoughts, feelings, and behaviors. CBT posits that the way we think significantly influences how we feel and act. This theory suggests that by consciously selecting and focusing on positive thoughts, we have the power to alter our emotional state and, consequently, our behaviors.

Affirmations serve as a practical application of this theory. When we engage in the deliberate practice of repeating positive statements, we are essentially taking control of our internal

6

dialogue. This process allows us to counteract and gradually replace negative or self-defeating thoughts with more constructive, empowering beliefs. The repetition of affirmations isn't just a superficial exercise; it plays a crucial role in the neurological process of "rewiring" the brain.

Neuroscientific research supports the idea that our brains are malleable, capable of forming new neural connections—a concept known as neuroplasticity. By consistently repeating affirmations, we reinforce positive thought patterns, which over time, can become ingrained in our subconscious mind. This rewiring process helps to diminish the impact of deeply entrenched negative beliefs, making way for a more optimistic and resilient mindset.

The impact of affirmations extends beyond mere positive thinking; they create a ripple effect on our overall mental health. As we replace negative thoughts with positive affirmations, we experience a shift in our emotional responses, leading to more positive behaviors and interactions with the world around us. This transformation not only enhances our self-esteem and confidence but also empowers us to face challenges with a more hopeful and constructive outlook. Through the consistent practice of affirmations, we harness the ability to reshape our mental and emotional landscape, paving the way for lasting personal growth and well-being.

How Affirmations Work

When you engage in the practice of repeating an affirmation, you are doing more than simply speaking words into existence;

you are actively reinforcing the neural pathways in your brain that are linked to those specific thoughts. This reinforcement process is crucial because it strengthens the connections between neurons associated with the positive statement, making those thoughts more readily accessible and influential in your day-to-day thinking. The brain's remarkable ability to adapt and reorganize itself, known as neuroplasticity, plays a central role in this transformation.

As you consistently repeat an affirmation, the neural pathways associated with that thought become increasingly robust, embedding the idea more deeply into your cognitive framework. This repetition isn't just a superficial activity; it gradually alters the landscape of your mind, leading to meaningful changes in your beliefs, attitudes, and ultimately, your behavior. Over time, the positive messages conveyed through your affirmations start to replace old, negative thought patterns, shifting your mental and emotional state toward a more positive outlook.

The key to this process lies in consistency and genuine belief in the truth of the affirmation. Repeating an affirmation without truly believing in its potential can limit its effectiveness. However, when you fully commit to the affirmation and trust in its validity, you enable the statement to resonate more deeply within your subconscious mind. This deep-seated belief accelerates the process of embedding the positive statement into your psyche, where it can influence your thoughts and actions at a subconscious level.

With regular practice, affirmations can become an integral

part of your mental and emotional makeup, subtly guiding your decisions, shaping your responses to challenges, and nurturing a more confident and empowered version of yourself. Through this process, you not only change your thought patterns but also lay the groundwork for long-lasting personal growth and transformation.

Chapter 2: The Impact of Positive Affirmations on Mental Health

Reducing Anxiety and Depression

Research has increasingly demonstrated that positive affirmations can serve as a powerful tool in alleviating symptoms of anxiety and depression. These mental health conditions are often characterized by a persistent cycle of negative thinking, where individuals become trapped in a loop of self-doubt, fear, and hopelessness. This negative spiral not only deepens emotional distress but can also lead to a diminished sense of self-worth and capability. Positive affirmations offer a way to disrupt this cycle by shifting the focus from destructive thoughts to constructive, empowering ones.

When individuals consciously repeat affirmations such as "I am in control of my thoughts and emotions" or "I am capable of handling anything that comes my way," they engage in cognitive restructuring. This process involves replacing negative, automatic thoughts with positive alternatives, which can help to reframe one's perspective on challenging situations. By consistently focusing on these affirmations, individuals begin to internalize these positive messages, gradually altering their thought patterns.

Over time, this shift in thinking can lead to a reduction in feelings of helplessness and an increase in self-efficacy—the belief in one's ability to influence events and outcomes in their life. As these affirmations take root in the subconscious mind, they start to manifest in tangible ways, empowering individuals to approach life's challenges with greater confidence and resilience. The sense of control and capability fostered by affirmations can be particularly beneficial for those struggling with anxiety and depression, as it counters the overwhelming sense of powerlessness that often accompanies these conditions.

The repetition of positive affirmations helps to build a mental foundation of self-compassion and optimism, which are essential components of mental well-being. By regularly reinforcing these positive beliefs, individuals can create a more supportive and nurturing internal dialogue, which can significantly contribute to their overall mental health. This transformation, though gradual, can lead to lasting improvements in mood, outlook, and quality of life, making positive affirmations a valuable tool in the journey toward emotional healing and personal growth.

Enhancing Self-Esteem and Self-Worth

Self-esteem serves as the cornerstone of mental health, influencing how we perceive ourselves and our place in the world. A strong sense of self-esteem provides the emotional stability and resilience needed to navigate life's challenges. Positive affirmations are an effective tool for nurturing and enhancing self-esteem, particularly when focusing on self-love, acceptance, and worthiness. By regularly repeating affirmations such as "I am worthy of love and respect" or "I am enough just as I am," individuals can begin to challenge and transform the negative beliefs that often undermine their self-worth.

These affirmations act as a powerful counterbalance to the internal criticism and self-doubt that many people experience. In a society that often imposes unrealistic standards and pressures, it's easy to internalize feelings of inadequacy or unworthiness. Positive affirmations offer a way to break free from these harmful thought patterns by replacing them with affirmations that affirm one's inherent value and dignity.

The practice of repeating affirmations isn't just about wishful thinking; it's a deliberate and conscious effort to reprogram the mind. By consistently affirming messages of self-love and acceptance, individuals begin to internalize these positive statements, gradually altering their self-perception. Over time, these affirmations can lead to a significant shift in self-image, fostering a more compassionate and accepting relationship with oneself.

As these positive beliefs take root, they lay the groundwork for greater self-confidence. When individuals start to see themselves as deserving of love, respect, and acceptance, they become more empowered to pursue their goals, set healthy boundaries, and make choices that reflect their true worth. This growing sense of self-confidence is not just about feeling good in the moment; it's about cultivating a deep and enduring belief in one's own value, which can profoundly impact all areas of life.

In the long term, the consistent use of positive affirmations can contribute to a more positive and resilient self-image, making it easier to maintain mental and emotional well-being. By reinforcing the belief that one is enough just as they are, affirmations help individuals build a strong foundation of self-esteem, enabling them to face life's challenges with a sense of inner strength and assurance.

Building Resilience

Resilience—the capacity to recover quickly from adversity and adapt to life's challenges—is a critical trait for mental and emotional well-being. In the face of setbacks and difficulties, resilience enables individuals to maintain a sense of stability and purpose, allowing them to navigate turbulent times without being overwhelmed. Positive affirmations can play a pivotal role in cultivating and strengthening resilience by promoting a optimistic and determined mindset.

Affirmations are powerful because they shape the way we perceive and respond to challenges. When individuals regularly repeat statements like "I have the strength to overcome any obstacle" or "I grow stronger with every experience," they are not just reciting words; they are actively reconditioning their

minds to approach difficulties with confidence and perseverance. These affirmations serve as mental anchors, grounding
individuals in the belief that they possess the inner strength
and resources to handle whatever comes their way.

This practice of reinforcing a positive mindset through affirmations helps to build mental toughness over time—the ability
to remain focused and resilient even in the face of adversity.
By internalizing messages of strength and growth, individuals
develop a more proactive attitude toward challenges, viewing
them not as insurmountable barriers but as opportunities for
personal development and learning. This shift in perspective
is crucial, as it empowers individuals to approach life's difficulties with a sense of agency and determination rather than
fear and helplessness.

Affirmations that emphasize resilience also help to create a
self-fulfilling prophecy. As individuals continuously affirm
their ability to overcome obstacles and grow from their experiences, they begin to embody these qualities more fully in
their daily lives. This embodiment of resilience is reflected in
their actions, decisions, and overall approach to life, leading
to a more robust and enduring capacity to bounce back from
setbacks.

In essence, the consistent use of affirmations focused on
resilience does more than just provide temporary motivation;
it fundamentally alters the way individuals perceive and respond to challenges. By fostering a resilient mindset, these
affirmations contribute to the development of a stronger, more
adaptable self—one that is better equipped to navigate the

complexities of life with grace and strength. Through this process, individuals survive adversity and thrive, emerging from their experiences with greater wisdom, courage, and inner fortitude.

4

Chapter 3: Affirmations and Success

Cultivating a Success Mindset

Success is frequently shaped not just by one's skills or efforts but by the mindset that drives those abilities. While talent and hard work are undeniably important, the way we think and perceive ourselves plays an equally critical role in determining our outcomes. A positive mindset acts as the foundation upon which success is built, and this is where affirmations come into play. Positive affirmations are powerful tools that help cultivate a mindset conducive to success by reinforcing key attributes such as determination, confidence, and perseverance.

When individuals regularly affirm statements like "I am a successful person" or "I am capable of achieving my goals," they are engaging in a mental practice that shifts their focus away from self-doubt and fear. These affirmations counterbalance the negative thoughts that often arise when facing challenges or pursuing ambitious goals. By consistently repeating positive, success-oriented statements, individuals begin to internalize these messages, gradually replacing limiting beliefs with empowering ones.

This shift in focus is not just about thinking positively; it's about creating a deep-seated belief in one's potential for success. Affirmations help to rewire the brain, aligning thoughts and attitudes with the desired outcome. As individuals embrace the belief that they are capable, worthy, and destined for success, they start to approach their goals with greater confidence and resolve. This change in mindset can be transformative, leading to increased motivation, persistence, and a willingness to take the necessary risks to achieve their aspirations.

Additionally, a success-oriented mindset fostered by affirmations influences behavior. When people believe in their potential, they are more likely to take decisive actions, seek out opportunities, and persevere in the face of setbacks. This proactive attitude creates a positive feedback loop, where the belief in success leads to actions that bring success closer to reality, further reinforcing the initial positive mindset.

In essence, positive affirmations are more than just words; they are catalysts for developing a mindset that embraces and attracts success. By focusing on affirmations that highlight determination, confidence, and perseverance, individuals can transform their inner dialogue, paving the way for a more empowered and success-driven outlook. This mental transformation not only enhances their chances of achieving their goals but also fosters a resilient and proactive approach to life, ensuring that success becomes a natural extension of their mindset and efforts.

Goal Setting and Achievement

Affirmations can be an incredibly effective tool in the process of goal setting and achievement, serving as a constant reminder of your intentions and helping to solidify your commitment to your aspirations. The power of affirmations lies in their ability to keep your goals at the forefront of your mind, consistently reinforcing their importance and your dedication to them. By repeatedly affirming statements like "I am committed to my goals and work towards them every day" or "I have the power to turn my dreams into reality," you are acknowledging your goals and cultivating the mindset necessary to achieve them.

This practice of affirming your goals helps to build a mental framework that prioritizes and values the steps needed to reach your objectives. When you consistently remind yourself of your commitment, it becomes easier to stay focused and motivated, even in the face of challenges or setbacks. Repetitioning affirmations embeds these positive beliefs into your subconscious, gradually shifting your thinking patterns from doubt and procrastination to determination and proactive action.

Affirmations serve as a source of inspiration and encouragement, especially when progress seems slow or obstacles arise. They act as a mental reinforcement, reminding you that you have the inner strength and resilience to overcome difficulties and stay on course. This consistent reinforcement helps to sustain your motivation, making it more likely that you will persist in your efforts and take the necessary actions to achieve your goals.

In addition to maintaining focus and motivation, affirmations also play a role in shaping your overall outlook on the goal-setting process. By affirming your ability to achieve your dreams, you foster a sense of self-efficacy and confidence, which are crucial for success. This positive mindset influences your behavior and attracts opportunities and resources that can support your journey toward your goals.

Ultimately, the regular use of affirmations in goal setting enhances your chances of success by aligning your thoughts, emotions, and actions with your aspirations. You create a powerful mental environment that supports and propels you to realize your dreams by consistently affirming your commitment and belief in your ability to achieve your goals. This mental conditioning ensures that your goals remain a priority in your life, guiding your decisions and actions toward successful outcomes.

Overcoming Procrastination and Doubt

Procrastination and self-doubt are two of the most common and formidable barriers to achieving success. They can create a paralyzing cycle where fear and uncertainty prevent you from taking the necessary steps toward your goals. The longer you delay action, the more entrenched these feelings can become, making it even harder to break free. However, positive affirmations offer a powerful strategy for overcoming these obstacles by shifting your mental focus away from negative thoughts and towards constructive, decisive action.

Affirmations such as "I take action now, without hesitation" or "I trust in my abilities and make decisions confidently" serve as direct countermeasures to procrastination and self-doubt. When you repeatedly affirm these positive statements, you are actively reprogramming your mind to prioritize action and confidence over delay and uncertainty. These affirmations help to replace the habitual thoughts that fuel procrastination—such as fear of failure or perfectionism—with empowering beliefs that encourage immediate and confident action.

The effectiveness of affirmations lies in their ability to change the internal narrative that governs your behavior. Instead of being trapped in a cycle of overthinking and inaction, affirmations encourage a mindset of proactivity and self-assurance. By consistently repeating affirmations that emphasize taking action and trusting in your abilities, you gradually begin to embody these qualities. This shift in mindset can profoundly impact your ability to overcome procrastination as you start to approach tasks with a sense of urgency and purpose rather than hesitation and doubt.

Affirmations that focus on confidence and decision-making help to strengthen your belief in your own capabilities. When you affirm statements like "I trust in my abilities," you reinforce the idea that you have the skills and knowledge needed to make sound decisions and achieve your goals. This increased self-trust reduces the tendency to second-guess yourself and empowers you to take bold and decisive actions, even in the face of uncertainty.

In the long run, the regular use of affirmations can lead to significant changes in behavior and mindset. By cultivating a habit of taking immediate action and trusting in your abilities, you become more adept at overcoming procrastination and self-doubt. This mental and behavioral transformation opens the door to greater productivity, efficiency, and ultimately, success. Affirmations, therefore, serve as a valuable tool in breaking the cycle of inaction, helping you to move forward with confidence and clarity toward your goals.

5

Chapter 4: The Role of Affirmations in Relationships

Improving Communication

Positive affirmations have the power to transform communication within relationships by cultivating a more positive, respectful, and empathetic attitude. The way we communicate greatly influences the quality of our relationships, and affirmations can serve as valuable tools to enhance this aspect of our interactions. By consciously affirming statements such as "I listen to others with an open heart" or "I communicate with clarity and kindness," individuals can develop a mindset that prioritizes understanding, empathy, and respect in every conversation.

Listening with an open heart is crucial for effective communication. When you affirm this intention, you are reminding yourself to approach each interaction with genuine interest and compassion. This means being fully present in the moment, giving the other person your undivided attention, and making an effort to truly understand their perspective. Over time, this practice can lead to deeper connections, as the people you interact with will feel heard and valued. This affirmation helps to counteract the tendency to listen only to respond, encouraging a more thoughtful and empathetic approach to communication.

In addition to enhancing your listening skills, affirmations that focus on clarity and kindness in communication can also greatly improve the way you express yourself. Clear and kind communication is the foundation of healthy personal or professional relationships. By affirming, "I communicate with clarity and kindness," you are setting the intention to speak in a way that is both understandable and considerate of others' feelings. This can help to reduce misunderstandings, prevent conflicts, and create a more harmonious environment in which all parties feel respected and valued.

The consistent use of these affirmations not only reinforces positive communication habits but also gradually reshapes your overall approach to relationships. As you internalize these affirmations, you may naturally adopt a more constructive and compassionate attitude in your interactions. This shift in mindset fosters an environment where open, honest, and empathetic communication can thrive, leading to stronger and more meaningful connections with others.

Ultimately, the impact of positive affirmations on communication is profound. By encouraging a focus on listening with empathy and expressing oneself with clarity and kindness, affirmations help to build a foundation of mutual respect and understanding in relationships. This, in turn, leads to more effective and fulfilling interactions, as both parties feel heard, valued, and connected. Over time, these enhanced communication skills can lead to stronger, more resilient relationships, grounded in trust, empathy, and mutual respect.

Strengthening Emotional Bonds

Affirmations centered on love and connection have the profound ability to deepen and strengthen emotional bonds between partners, friends, and family members. These affirmations act as a continual reminder of the value and significance of nurturing relationships, fostering a greater sense of appreciation and closeness. By affirming statements like "I nurture my relationships with love and care" or "Loving and supportive people surround me," individuals actively reinforce the emotional fabric that binds them to others.

When you consistently repeat affirmations emphasizing nurturing relationships with love and care, you cultivate a mindset prioritizing emotional investment and mutual support. This intentional focus helps you to recognize and value the effort required to maintain and enhance your connections with those you care about. By affirming your commitment to loving and caring for others, you are more likely to engage in behaviors that strengthen these bonds, such as offering support, expressing appreciation, and being present in the moment.

Additionally, affirmations that highlight the presence of loving and supportive people in your life help to foster a sense of gratitude and acknowledgment. Statements like "Loving and supportive people surround me" encourage you to recognize and appreciate the positive relationships that enrich your life. This sense of gratitude can lead to more meaningful interactions and a greater appreciation for the role that supportive individuals play in your well-being.

As you internalize these affirmations, they become a guiding force in how you approach your relationships. You may find yourself more attuned to the emotional needs of others and more proactive in expressing your affection and support. This shift in mindset not only enhances the quality of your interactions but also contributes to a more resilient and harmonious emotional network.

The practice of using affirmations focused on love and connection strengthens the bonds between you and those around you by reinforcing the importance of emotional engagement and mutual support. By nurturing your relationships with intentional care and recognizing the loving presence of others in your life, you create a foundation of trust, appreciation, and emotional security. This enriched sense of connection deepens your relationships and contributes to a more fulfilling and supportive social environment.

Enhancing Self-Love and Self-Acceptance

Before one can truly offer love and support to others, it is crucial to first cultivate a deep sense of self-love and self-acceptance. This internal foundation of self-worth is not only essential for personal well-being but also significantly influences the quality of our relationships with others. Positive affirmations play a vital role in fostering this self-love by consistently reinforcing a positive self-image and nurturing a profound sense of self-respect.

Affirmations such as "I am deserving of love and respect" and "I honor and accept myself completely" serve as powerful tools in this process. These statements are more than mere words; they are deliberate practices that help individuals internalize a sense of intrinsic value and self-worth. When you affirm that you deserve love and respect, you actively challenge and reshape any negative beliefs or self-doubt that may have previously hindered your self-esteem. This affirmation encourages you to acknowledge and embrace your worthiness, laying the groundwork for healthier and more fulfilling interactions with others.

Similarly, affirming "I honor and accept myself completely" promotes a comprehensive sense of self-acceptance. This affirmation encourages you to embrace all aspects of yourself—both strengths and imperfections—without judgment. By honoring yourself in this way, you build a foundation of self-love that allows you to approach relationships with greater confidence and authenticity.

Cultivating self-love through affirmations enhances your self-perception and positively impacts how you relate to others. When you have a strong sense of self-worth, you are more likely to engage in relationships from a place of confidence and security rather than seeking validation or approval. This shift enables you to offer love and support to others more freely, as your self-love serves as a wellspring from which you can draw compassion and empathy.

The practice of self-love through affirmations helps to create a solid internal foundation that enriches your relationships with others. By affirming your own value and embracing self-acceptance, you prepare yourself to engage with others in a more meaningful and balanced way. This self-love not only enhances your own well-being but also fosters healthier, more supportive connections with those around you, ultimately leading to more harmonious and fulfilling relationships.

Chapter 5: Affirmations and Physical Health

The Mind-Body Connection

The concept of the mind-body connection is a cornerstone of both traditional and modern medicine, highlighting the profound impact that mental states can have on physical health. This intricate relationship between the mind and body suggests that our thoughts, emotions, and beliefs can directly influence various bodily functions and overall well-being. Positive affirmations are a powerful tool in this dynamic, offering a method to enhance physical health by fostering a positive and constructive mental state.

Affirmations promote a mindset that supports physical well-being and reduces stress, which is known to harm health. When chronic, stress can weaken the immune system, disrupt bodily functions, and contribute to various health issues. By using positive affirmations such as "My body is healthy, strong, and full of energy," individuals can actively shift their focus towards a positive outlook on their physical health. This shift helps to counteract negative thoughts that may contribute to stress and can lead to improved bodily functions.

The power of affirmations extends beyond stress reduction. Positive affirmations can boost the immune system by reinforcing a belief in the body's ability to heal and remain resilient. When individuals repeatedly affirm their health and vitality, they are more likely to engage in behaviors that support their well-being, such as maintaining a healthy diet, exercising regularly, and getting adequate rest. Fueled by a positive mindset, this proactive approach enhances the body's natural defenses and contributes to overall health.

Furthermore, affirmations help cultivate a deeper sense of self-awareness and self-care. By regularly affirming statements that reflect a positive view of one's health, individuals become more attuned to their body's needs and are more motivated to take actions that support their physical well-being. This enhanced self-awareness can lead to more mindful choices and behaviors, contributing to a healthier lifestyle.

Integrating positive affirmations into daily life can significantly impact physical health by reinforcing a positive mindset, reducing stress, and encouraging behaviors that support overall well-being. By affirming one's health and vitality, individuals strengthen the mind-body connection, improving bodily functions and a greater sense of physical and emotional balance.

Stress Reduction

Stress is a pervasive and significant factor in a myriad of health issues, ranging from chronic conditions to acute ailments. Its effects on the body can be profound, leading to increased susceptibility to illness, impaired immune function, and a general decline in overall well-being. One of the most effective ways to manage and mitigate the impact of stress is through the use of positive affirmations, which can serve as a powerful tool for fostering a sense of calm and control.

Positive affirmations work by shifting the focus from stress-inducing thoughts to calming and empowering statements that promote relaxation and mental clarity. When individuals consistently repeat affirmations such as "I release all tension from my body and mind" or "I am calm, relaxed, and in control," they are actively cultivating a mindset that counters the effects of stress. These affirmations help to reframe one's perception of stressful situations, reducing their emotional impact and encouraging a more balanced response.

Affirmations involve mentally engaging with positive statements, which can reduce the physiological symptoms of stress. For example, focusing on the affirmation "I release all tension from my body and mind" can help lower heart rate, reduce muscle tension, and promote a sense of physical relaxation. By consistently affirming a state of calm, individuals may also experience decreased anxiety levels and improved overall mood.

Positive affirmations can enhance one's sense of control over stress by reinforcing beliefs in personal resilience and coping abilities. Statements like "I am calm, relaxed, and in control" help individuals to view themselves as capable of handling stress effectively, thereby empowering them to navigate challenging situations with greater ease and confidence.

Incorporating positive affirmations into daily routines can create a mental environment that supports stress management and promotes relaxation. By regularly engaging with these empowering statements, individuals can cultivate a more resilient mindset, leading to improved emotional and physical well-being. This proactive approach to managing stress not only enhances one's ability to cope with daily pressures but also contributes to long-term health and vitality.

Encouraging Healthy Habits

Affirmations have a powerful role in encouraging and reinforcing the adoption of healthy habits, significantly impacting overall physical well-being. By consistently affirming positive behaviors, individuals can cultivate a mindset that supports and sustains a healthier lifestyle. Affirmations such as "I choose foods that nourish my body" or "I am committed to maintaining a healthy lifestyle" are not just statements but are tools for instilling and solidifying beneficial habits that contribute to long-term health.

When individuals repeat affirmations like "I choose foods that nourish my body," they reinforce the importance of making mindful and health-conscious choices in their diet. This affirmation encourages a focus on selecting nutritious foods that provide essential vitamins, minerals, and energy, rather than succumbing to less healthy options. Over time, this positive reinforcement helps to establish a habit of prioritizing wholesome, nourishing foods, leading to better dietary choices and improved physical health.

Similarly, affirmations such as "I am committed to maintaining a healthy lifestyle" foster a broader commitment to overall wellness. This statement encompasses not just dietary choices but also other aspects of health, such as regular physical activity, adequate sleep, and stress management. By affirming this commitment daily, individuals are more likely to engage in activities and make decisions that align with their health goals. This consistent reinforcement helps to integrate healthy behaviors into their routine, making them more habitual and less of a conscious effort.

The impact of these affirmations extends beyond immediate behavior changes. Individuals gradually shift their mindset towards a more health-focused perspective by continually affirming positive health-related statements. This mental shift can lead to lasting changes in lifestyle, as the affirmations help to create a self-reinforcing cycle of positive behaviors. Over time, these affirmations contribute to developing a healthier lifestyle, supporting sustained physical well-being and vitality.

Positive affirmations serve as a powerful catalyst for adopting and maintaining healthy habits. By consistently focusing on statements promoting nourishment and commitment to wellness, individuals can effectively reinforce behaviors that improve health outcomes. This approach encourages the development of beneficial habits and supports a positive and proactive attitude towards overall well-being.

7

Chapter 6: The Science Behind Positive Affirmations

Neuroplasticity and Affirmations

Neuroplasticity, the remarkable ability of the brain to reorganize and adapt by forming new neural connections, plays a crucial role in the effectiveness of positive affirmations. This dynamic process enables the brain to modify its structure and function in response to new experiences, thoughts, and behaviors. When individuals consistently repeat positive affirmations, they leverage neuroplasticity to strengthen and reinforce neural pathways associated with these affirmations, leading to lasting changes in their behavior and outlook.

Positive affirmations involve deliberately repeating constructive statements to influence one's mindset and actions. As these affirmations are repeated, they stimulate specific neural pathways in the brain, which are responsible for processing and reinforcing those positive thoughts. For instance, affirmations such as "I am confident and capable" or "I attract positivity into my life" engage neural circuits related to self-belief and optimism. The repetitive nature of affirmations helps to activate and strengthen these neural connections, making them more robust and efficient over time.

This process of reinforcing neural pathways through positive affirmations has significant implications for behavior and outlook. As the neural connections associated with affirmations become stronger, the thoughts and beliefs they represent become more ingrained in the individual's cognitive framework. This enhanced neural connectivity makes these positive thoughts more likely to influence behavior, decision-making, and overall perspective.

The impact of neuroplasticity extends beyond mere thought reinforcement. As neural pathways associated with positive affirmations become more established, they can help to replace negative or unproductive thought patterns with more constructive and empowering ones. This shift contributes to improved emotional regulation, increased self-esteem, and a more optimistic outlook on life.

Neuroplasticity underpins the effectiveness of positive affirmations by facilitating the formation and strengthening of neural connections associated with positive thoughts and beliefs. Through the repetitive practice of affirmations, individuals can harness this brain adaptability to influence their behavior and mindset, ultimately leading to meaningful and lasting changes in their overall outlook and well-being.

The Role of the Reticular Activating System (RAS)

The Reticular Activating System (RAS) is a vital network of neurons located in the brainstem that plays a key role in filtering and prioritizing the vast amount of sensory information we encounter every day. This system acts as a gatekeeper, determining which stimuli we consciously focus on and which are ignored. By influencing the RAS, affirmations can help to shift our attention toward positive thoughts and opportunities, effectively guiding our perceptions and actions.

The RAS highlights information aligning with our thoughts, beliefs, and goals. When we repeat positive affirmations, such as "I am open to new opportunities" or "I attract success and positivity," we actively engage in mental programming. These affirmations send clear signals to the RAS, directing it to prioritize and filter information that supports these positive statements. As a result, the RAS becomes more attuned to recognizing and seizing opportunities that align with our affirmations.

For example, if you frequently affirm that you are capable and deserving of success, your RAS will start to focus more on cues and situations that reflect this belief. This heightened awareness can increase motivation, confidence, and a more proactive approach to pursuing goals. Conversely, if negative self-talk prevails, the RAS will be more likely to filter in negative information and reinforce limiting beliefs.

By consistently practicing positive affirmations, individuals can reprogram the RAS to shift its focus from negative or self-limiting thoughts to constructive and empowering ones. This reprogramming enhances one's ability to recognize and act on opportunities, fostering a more positive and goal-oriented mindset. The influence of affirmations on the RAS underscores the profound impact that intentional thought patterns can have on shaping our experiences and outcomes in life.

The Reticular Activating System is a powerful tool for filtering and prioritizing information based on our focus and beliefs. By strategically using positive affirmations, individuals can effectively guide the RAS to concentrate on positive thoughts and opportunities, leading to a more fulfilling and successful life experience.

The Placebo Effect and Affirmations

The placebo effect is a compelling demonstration of belief and expectation's profound influence on physical and mental health outcomes. This phenomenon occurs when individuals experience real changes in their health after receiving a treatment that has no therapeutic value simply because they believe it will work. This effect underscores how powerful the mind can be in shaping our experiences and well-being. Similarly, positive affirmations harness this same principle by leveraging the power of belief to effect meaningful changes in one's life.

Positive affirmations involve intentionally repeating constructive and empowering statements, such as "I am capable of achieving my goals" or "I am worthy of success and happiness." The effectiveness of these affirmations is rooted in the principle that belief can influence reality. By consistently repeating these affirmations, individuals cultivate a strong belief in the truth of the statements they are affirming. This belief, much like the placebo effect, can trigger a cascade of mental and physical positive changes.

When individuals fully engage with affirmations, their belief in these positive statements shapes their attitudes, behaviors, and even physiological responses. This process can lead to improved self-confidence, enhanced motivation, and a more optimistic outlook on life. The mind's conviction in the truth of these affirmations can manifest in tangible ways, such as increased resilience to stress, better health outcomes, and a more proactive approach to goal achievement.

The power of belief, as illustrated by the placebo effect, highlights the importance of mental states in influencing our experiences. Positive affirmations leverage this power by reinforcing beneficial beliefs and attitudes, ultimately guiding individuals toward a more empowered and fulfilled state of being. Through the strategic use of affirmations, individuals can tap into the transformative potential of belief, fostering significant positive changes in their lives.

8

Chapter 7: Practical Application of Positive Affirmations

Crafting Effective Affirmations

Not all affirmations have the same impact; the effectiveness of an affirmation largely depends on how well it is crafted. In this chapter, we will delve into the essential principles for creating affirmations that are truly transformative. To maximize their effectiveness, affirmations should be personal, specific, and positive. By adhering to these guidelines, you can ensure that your affirmations resonate deeply with you and align with your goals.

First and foremost, affirmations should be personal. This means that the statements you create must be tailored to your unique circumstances, desires, and values. A personalized affirmation speaks directly to your individual aspirations and challenges, making it more relevant and powerful. For example, instead of a generic statement like "I am successful," a more personal affirmation might be "I am confidently pursuing my dream career and achieving my goals."

Specificity is another crucial element in crafting effective affirmations. Broad or vague statements are less likely to generate the desired impact. Specific affirmations provide clear, detailed, and actionable goals. For instance, rather than saying "I am healthy," a more specific affirmation could be "I am committed to exercising three times a week and eating balanced meals to enhance my energy and well-being."

Additionally, using the present tense is essential. Affirmations should be phrased as if the desired outcome is already happening. This approach helps to align your mindset with the reality you wish to create. For example, "I am confident and capable in all my endeavors" reinforces the belief that you are already embodying these qualities.

It is also important that the affirmation focuses on what you want, rather than what you don't want. Positive affirmations should concentrate on desirable outcomes and aspirations, avoiding negative phrasing. For instance, instead of "I am not afraid of public speaking," a more effective affirmation would be "I am confident and articulate when speaking in public."

Finally, for an affirmation to be truly effective, it must resonate with you emotionally. An affirmation that evokes a strong emotional response is more likely to influence your thoughts and actions. Choose statements that inspire, motivate, and connect with your core values and desires.

By following these guidelines—personalizing your affirmations, being specific, using the present tense, focusing on positive outcomes, and ensuring emotional resonance—you can create powerful affirmations that drive meaningful change and foster a more positive and empowered mindset.

Incorporating Affirmations into Daily Life

Incorporating affirmations into your daily routine is crucial for maximizing their effectiveness and harnessing their full potential. To truly benefit from affirmations, they need to be a consistent and integral part of your everyday life. This section will explore a variety of methods to seamlessly weave affirmations into your daily activities, enhancing their impact and ensuring they become a natural part of your routine.

One effective way to integrate affirmations is by writing them in a journal. Keeping a dedicated affirmation journal allows you to document your chosen affirmations and reflect on their meaning each day. Start by writing down your affirmations in the morning, setting a positive tone for the day. You can also use the journal to track your progress and note any changes in your thoughts or behaviors as a result of these affirmations. This reflective practice reinforces the affirmations and helps you stay connected to your goals.

Repeating affirmations aloud is another powerful method. Verbal repetition engages both the mind and body, reinforcing the positive statements through auditory and vocal channels. Choose a quiet moment in your day, such as during your morning routine or while getting ready for bed, to repeat your affirmations aloud. The act of speaking the affirmations can deepen your commitment to them and help embed them into your subconscious mind.

Using visual reminders can also be highly effective in keeping affirmations at the forefront of your consciousness. Place affirmation cards or sticky notes with your positive statements in prominent locations, such as on your bathroom mirror, refrigerator door, or workspace. These visual cues serve as constant reminders of your affirmations, ensuring that you regularly encounter and engage with them throughout the day.

Incorporating affirmations into specific daily practices, such as morning routines and bedtime rituals, can further enhance their effectiveness. For instance, start your day with a brief affirmation practice—recite your affirmations while sipping your morning coffee or during your commute. Similarly, end your day with a calming affirmation session as part of your bedtime routine, perhaps while unwinding with a book or preparing for sleep.

By exploring and implementing these various methods—journaling, verbal repetition, visual reminders, and integrating affirmations into daily routines—you can create a consistent practice that reinforces the positive messages and helps you achieve lasting change. Making affirmations a regular part of your daily life will make them a powerful tool for personal growth and transformation.

Overcoming Common Challenges

Starting an affirmation practice can be both empowering and

challenging. Many individuals struggle to maintain consistency or fully believe in their affirmations, particularly in the initial stages. This chapter will delve into these common challenges and offer practical strategies to overcome them, ensuring a successful and sustainable affirmation practice.

One of the primary obstacles is skepticism. When beginning an affirmation practice, it's not uncommon to question the effectiveness of repeating positive statements, especially if past attempts at self-improvement haven't yielded the desired results. To address this skepticism, it's essential to approach affirmations with an open mind and patience. Understanding that change takes time can help alleviate doubts. Begin by setting realistic expectations and acknowledging small victories along the way. Track your progress and reflect on any subtle shifts in your mindset or behavior, even if they initially seem minor.

Lack of motivation is another common hurdle. Maintaining enthusiasm for your affirmation practice can be challenging, particularly when immediate results aren't apparent. To combat this, integrate affirmations into your daily routine in a natural and enjoyable way. Consider pairing affirmations with other positive habits, such as a morning coffee or a nightly relaxation ritual, to create a sense of routine and reward. Additionally, revisiting and refreshing your affirmations regularly can keep them relevant and inspiring.

Staying committed to an affirmation practice requires discipline and adaptability. To enhance consistency, set specific times each day for your affirmation practice and treat them as non-negotiable appointments with yourself. Use tools such as reminder alarms or affirmation journals to keep you on track. As your life evolves and circumstances change, it's important to adapt your affirmations to reflect your current goals and challenges. Periodically review and revise your affirmations to ensure they align with your evolving aspirations and personal growth.

By addressing these challenges head-on and employing strategies to maintain motivation and adaptability, you can cultivate a robust affirmation practice that supports your personal development and helps you achieve lasting change. Embracing these practices with commitment and flexibility will pave the way for a more positive and transformative experience with affirmations.

9

Chapter 8: 365 Days of Positive Affirmations and Reflection Questions

This chapter is your daily companion, offering 365 affirmations designed to uplift, inspire, and empower you. Each affirmation is paired with a thought-provoking reflection question, encouraging you to delve deeper into your thoughts, beliefs, and experiences.

In today's fast-paced world, getting caught up in negativity and self-doubt is easy. Affirmations serve as powerful tools to counter these influences, helping you to cultivate a mindset focused on happiness, success, and personal growth. Regularly engaging with these affirmations and reflecting on the accompanying questions will rewire your thinking patterns, strengthen your self-belief, and unlock your full potential.

This chapter is more than just a collection of words—it's a daily practice. As you read an affirmation and ponder the question, take a moment to internalize its message each day. Allow the positive energy to resonate within you, guiding you towards a more fulfilling and purposeful life. To further enhance the effectiveness of your affirmations, consider using a notebook or journal to write them down along with your reflections. This practice not only helps you stay organized but also deepens your engagement with the positive changes you're striving for. Whether you're looking to boost your confidence, achieve your goals, or simply find more joy in everyday moments, these affirmations and reflections support you every step of the way.

Day 1: Affirmation for Wealth

Affirmation: "I am open to receiving abundance in all areas of my life."

Explanation: Being open to abundance is the first step toward attracting wealth. This affirmation helps you cultivate a mindset that welcomes prosperity, recognizing that abundance can manifest in various forms.

Reflection Questions:

1. In what ways did you open yourself to receiving abundance today?
2. How does your mindset about wealth and abundance affect your financial situation?
3. What steps can you take to create more opportunities for abundance?

Day 2: Affirmation for Love

Affirmation: "I give and receive love effortlessly and joyfully."

Explanation: Love flows freely when you approach it with openness and joy. This affirmation encourages a balanced exchange of love, where giving and receiving are equally important and fulfilling.

Reflection Questions:

1. How did you give and receive love today?
2. What makes it easy for you to express and accept love?
3. How can you enhance the flow of love in your relationships?

Day 3: Affirmation for Purpose

Affirmation: "I am clear about my purpose, and I pursue it with passion."

Explanation: Clarity and passion are essential for living a purposeful life. This affirmation strengthens your commitment to understanding and following your purpose, infusing your actions with enthusiasm.

Reflection Questions:

1. How clear are you about your purpose?
2. What actions did you take today that were aligned with your purpose?
3. How can you deepen your passion for pursuing your

47

purpose?

Day 4: Affirmation for Self-Confidence

Affirmation: "I trust in my abilities and confidently pursue my goals."

Explanation: Self-confidence comes from trusting in your abilities and knowing that you have what it takes to achieve your goals. This affirmation boosts your belief in yourself and encourages you to move forward with confidence.

Reflection Questions:

1. How did you demonstrate confidence in yourself today?
2. What abilities do you trust the most, and how do they help you achieve your goals?
3. What can you do to build even more confidence in your abilities?

Day 5: Affirmation for Positivity

Affirmation: "I choose to focus on the positive in every situation."

Explanation: Your outlook on life is shaped by where you focus your attention. This affirmation helps you maintain a positive mindset by consciously choosing to see the good in every circumstance.

Reflection Questions:

1. What positive aspects did you focus on today?
2. How did choosing positivity impact your day?
3. What strategies can you use to maintain a positive focus in challenging situations?

Day 6: Affirmation for Security

Affirmation: "I am safe, secure, and protected in all that I do."

Explanation: A sense of security is fundamental to well-being. This affirmation reinforces your belief that you are safe and protected, allowing you to navigate life with confidence and peace of mind.

Reflection Questions:

1. How did you experience a sense of security today?
2. What contributes to your feelings of safety and protection?
3. How can you strengthen your sense of security in your daily life?

Day 7: Affirmation for Happiness

Affirmation: "I choose to focus on the positives in my life and let go of negativity."

Explanation: Happiness often comes from what you focus on. By consciously choosing to see the good in every situation, you allow yourself to experience more joy. Letting go of negativity creates space for positivity to flourish.

Reflection Questions:

1. What positive things happened today that you can focus on?
2. How did letting go of a negative thought or situation make you feel?
3. How can you practice this mindset daily?

Day 8: Affirmation for Purpose

Affirmation: "I am clear about my purpose and take steps daily to fulfill it."

Explanation: Clarity of purpose gives your life direction. This affirmation encourages you to stay focused on your goals and take consistent action towards them, knowing that each step brings you closer to your purpose.

Reflection Questions:

1. What steps did you take today to move closer to your purpose?

2. How does being clear about your purpose influence your decisions?
3. What obstacles might be hindering your clarity, and how can you overcome them?

Day 9: Affirmation for Success

Affirmation: "I am worthy of success and embrace it in all areas of my life."

Explanation: Success starts with believing you deserve it. This affirmation helps to cultivate a mindset that welcomes success, recognizing that you are capable and deserving of achieving your goals.

Reflection Questions:

1. In what areas of your life do you feel most successful?
2. How can you apply this feeling of worthiness to other areas where you seek success?
3. What is one step you can take today to further embrace your success?

Day 10: Affirmation for Wealth

Affirmation: "I attract wealth and prosperity with ease."

Explanation: Wealth can flow effortlessly into your life when you believe it is possible. This affirmation encourages a mindset that naturally attracts financial abundance without struggle or resistance.

Reflection Questions:

1. How did you attract wealth and prosperity today?
2. What beliefs about money support your financial success?
3. What can you do to align more with the energy of effortless abundance?

Day 11: Affirmation for Love

Affirmation: "I am worthy of deep, fulfilling love."

Explanation: Believing in your worthiness is key to attracting and maintaining a loving relationship. This affirmation helps you recognize that you deserve deep, meaningful connections.

Reflection Questions:

1. How did you affirm your worthiness of love today?
2. What does fulfilling love mean to you, and how can you cultivate it?
3. How can you show yourself more love and appreciation?

Day 12: Affirmation for Purpose

Affirmation: "My purpose inspires me to take bold and meaningful action."

Explanation: Purpose-driven actions are often bold and impactful. This affirmation motivates you to take significant steps toward your goals, driven by the inspiration your purpose provides.

Reflection Questions:

1. What bold actions did you take today that were inspired by your purpose?
2. How does your purpose motivate you to make meaningful decisions?
3. What can you do to ensure your actions remain aligned with your purpose?

Day 13: Affirmation for Self-Confidence

Affirmation: "I am confident in who I am and embrace my uniqueness."

Explanation: Confidence grows when you fully accept and celebrate your individuality. This affirmation encourages you to embrace what makes you unique, knowing that your distinct qualities are strengths.

Reflection Questions:

1. How did you embrace your uniqueness today?

2. In what ways did you feel confident in being yourself?

3. What unique qualities do you want to celebrate more often?

Day 14: Affirmation for Positivity

Affirmation: "I radiate positivity and attract positive experiences."

Explanation: Positivity is contagious and has the power to attract good experiences into your life. This affirmation encourages you to radiate positive energy, drawing more of the same into your life.

Reflection Questions:

1. How did you radiate positivity today?

2. What positive experiences did you attract as a result?

3. How can you continue to be a source of positivity for yourself and others?

Day 15: Affirmation for Security

Affirmation: "I create a life of stability and security."

Explanation: Security often comes from creating a stable foundation in your life. This affirmation empowers you to take control of your circumstances, building a life that feels safe and secure.

Reflection Questions:

1. What steps did you take today to create stability in your life?
2. How does stability contribute to your overall sense of security?
3. What areas of your life could benefit from more stability?

Day 16: Affirmation for Happiness

Affirmation: "I create my own happiness by making choices that align with my values."

Explanation: True happiness comes from living in alignment with your core values. This affirmation encourages you to make choices that resonate with who you are, leading to a more fulfilling and joyful life.

Reflection Questions:

1. What choices did you make today that aligned with your values?
2. How did these choices impact your sense of happiness?
3. Are there areas in your life where you can better align your actions with your values?

Day 17: Affirmation for Purpose

Affirmation: "I am passionate about my purpose, and it drives me to achieve great things."

Explanation: Passion fuels purpose. When you are passionate about what you do, it becomes easier to stay motivated and push through challenges. This affirmation reminds you to keep your passion alive as you pursue your goals.

Reflection Questions:

1. What passions drive you towards your purpose?
2. How did your passion influence your actions today?
3. What can you do to nurture your passion and keep it strong?

Day 18: Affirmation for Success

Affirmation: "I am disciplined, focused, and persistent in achieving my goals."

Explanation: Success often requires discipline, focus, and persistence. This affirmation helps to reinforce these qualities, reminding you that consistency in your efforts will lead to the results you desire.

Reflection Questions:

1. How did you demonstrate discipline and focus today?
2. What challenges did you face, and how did persistence help you overcome them?

3. How can you maintain these qualities as you continue working toward your goals?

Day 19: Affirmation for Wealth

Affirmation: "I manage my finances wisely and am in control of my financial destiny."

Explanation: Wise financial management is crucial for building wealth. This affirmation reinforces your ability to make sound financial decisions, putting you in control of your economic future.

Reflection Questions:

1. How did you manage your finances today?
2. What financial decisions are you proud of?
3. What steps can you take to improve your financial management further?

Day 20: Affirmation for Love

Affirmation: "My heart is open to giving and receiving unconditional love."

Explanation: Unconditional love is the purest form of love, free from judgment or expectation. This affirmation helps you cultivate an open heart, ready to give and receive love without conditions.

Reflection Questions:

1. How did you give or receive unconditional love today?
2. What does unconditional love mean to you?
3. How can you practice more unconditional love in your relationships?

Day 21: Affirmation for Purpose

Affirmation: "Every day, I move closer to fulfilling my true purpose."

Explanation: Progress toward your purpose can be achieved through consistent daily actions. This affirmation motivates you to keep moving forward, knowing that each step brings you closer to fulfilling your purpose.

Reflection Questions:

1. What did you do today to move closer to your purpose?
2. How do you measure your progress toward your purpose?
3. What can you do tomorrow to continue advancing toward your goals?

Day 22: Affirmation for Self-Confidence

Affirmation: "I believe in myself and my ability to succeed."

Explanation: Success begins with self-belief. This affirmation reinforces your confidence in your capabilities, encouraging you to pursue your goals with the assurance that you will succeed.

Reflection Questions:

1. How did you show belief in yourself today?
2. What successes have you achieved by trusting in your abilities?
3. How can you continue to build your self-belief?

Day 23: Affirmation for Positivity

Affirmation: "I approach life with optimism and an open heart."

Explanation: An optimistic attitude opens the door to positive experiences. This affirmation encourages you to approach life with hope and a willingness to embrace new opportunities.

Reflection Questions:

1. How did you demonstrate optimism today?
2. What positive experiences came from keeping an open heart?
3. How can you maintain optimism in the face of challenges?

Day 24: Affirmation for Security

Affirmation: "I trust that everything in my life is working out for my highest good."

Explanation: Trusting in the process of life brings a deep sense of security. This affirmation helps you feel secure by reinforcing your belief that everything is unfolding for your ultimate benefit.

Reflection Questions:

1. How did you trust in the process of life today?
2. What evidence have you seen that things are working out for your highest good?
3. How can you strengthen your trust in the unfolding of your life?

Day 25: Affirmation for Happiness

Affirmation: "I am grateful for the abundance in my life and welcome more joy every day."

Explanation: Gratitude is a powerful tool for happiness. By focusing on the abundance you already have, you open yourself up to even more joy. This affirmation encourages you to practice gratitude daily.

Reflection Questions:

1. What are you most grateful for today?
2. How does practicing gratitude impact your overall happiness?

3. What new ways can you incorporate gratitude into your daily routine?

Day 26: Affirmation for Purpose

Affirmation: "I am guided by my intuition and trust the path I am on."

Explanation: Trusting your intuition can lead you closer to your purpose. This affirmation encourages you to listen to your inner voice and trust that it's guiding you toward the right path, even when the way forward isn't clear.

Reflection Questions:

1. How did your intuition guide you today?
2. What decisions did you make based on your inner guidance?
3. How can you strengthen your connection to your intuition?

Day 27: Affirmation for Success

Affirmation: "I am open to new opportunities and embrace them with confidence."

Explanation: Success often comes from seizing opportunities. This affirmation encourages you to be open to new possibilities and approach them with confidence, knowing they can lead to growth and success.

Reflection Questions:

1. What new opportunities did you encounter today?
2. How did you approach these opportunities with confidence?
3. How can you stay open to future possibilities?

Day 28: Affirmation for Wealth

Affirmation: "I am worthy of financial success and abundance."

Explanation: Recognizing your worth is key to attracting financial success. This affirmation helps you internalize the belief that you deserve abundance and financial prosperity.

Reflection Questions:

1. How did you affirm your worthiness of financial success today?
2. What beliefs might be holding you back from fully embracing your financial potential?
3. How can you reinforce your sense of worthiness when it comes to wealth?

Day 29: Affirmation for Love

Affirmation: "I am surrounded by love and positive energy."

Explanation: When you focus on love and positivity, you attract more of it into your life. This affirmation reminds you to recognize the love and positive energy that already exists around you and to attract even more.

Reflection Questions:

1. How did you feel surrounded by love and positive energy today?
2. In what ways did you contribute to the loving and positive energy around you?
3. How can you continue to cultivate an environment filled with love and positivity?

Day 30: Affirmation for Purpose

Affirmation: "My life is filled with meaning and purpose, and I align my actions accordingly."

Explanation: When your actions are aligned with your purpose, your life takes on greater meaning. This affirmation encourages you to stay true to your purpose and make decisions that reflect your deeper values.

Reflection Questions:

1. How did you align your actions with your purpose today?
2. What aspects of your life feel most meaningful to you?

3. What steps can you take to ensure your daily actions continue to reflect your purpose?

Day 31: Affirmation for Self-Confidence

Affirmation: "I am proud of who I am becoming."

Explanation: Confidence grows when you acknowledge and celebrate your personal growth. This affirmation encourages you to take pride in your journey, recognizing the positive changes you are making.

Reflection Questions:

1. What aspects of yourself are you proud of today?
2. How have you grown recently, and what changes have you noticed in yourself?
3. How can you continue to cultivate pride in your personal development?

Day 32: Affirmation for Positivity

Affirmation: "I see the good in every situation and learn from every experience."

Explanation: Positivity often comes from the ability to find lessons in all experiences, both good and bad. This affirmation encourages you to seek the good in every situation and use it as an opportunity for growth.

Reflection Questions:

1. What positive lessons did you learn today?
2. How did focusing on the good change your perspective on a challenging situation?
3. How can you make it a habit to find the positive in every experience?

Day 33: Affirmation for Security

Affirmation: "I am grounded, centered, and secure in who I am."

Explanation: Feeling secure begins with being grounded and centered within yourself. This affirmation helps you cultivate a strong inner foundation, providing a sense of stability and security.

Reflection Questions:

1. How did you feel grounded and centered today?
2. What practices help you stay connected to your inner sense of security?
3. How can you strengthen your grounding and centering practices?

Day 34: Affirmation for Happiness

Affirmation: "I release what no longer serves me and welcome peace into my life."

Explanation: Holding onto things that no longer serve you can block your happiness. This affirmation encourages you to let go of anything that's weighing you down, creating space for peace and contentment.

Reflection Questions:

1. What did you release today that no longer serves you?
2. How did this act of letting go affect your sense of peace?
3. Are there other areas in your life where you need to release negativity?

Day 35: Affirmation for Purpose

Affirmation: "I am a creative force, and my purpose is expressed through my unique talents."

Explanation: Your creativity is a key part of your purpose. This affirmation reminds you that your unique talents and ideas are valuable and that expressing them is an essential part of fulfilling your purpose.

Reflection Questions:

1. How did you express your creativity today?
2. How does your creativity connect to your sense of purpose?

3. What can you do to further cultivate and express your talents?

Day 36: Affirmation for Success

Affirmation: "I believe in my ability to create the life I desire."

Explanation: Success begins with belief in yourself. This affirmation reinforces the idea that you have the power to shape your life and achieve your dreams, starting with a strong belief in your capabilities.

Reflection Questions:

1. How did you demonstrate belief in yourself today?
2. What actions did you take to create the life you desire?
3. How can you strengthen your self-belief going forward?

Day 37: Affirmation for Wealth

Affirmation: "I am a magnet for financial opportunities."

Explanation: Financial opportunities arise when you are open and ready to receive them. This affirmation helps you attract wealth by becoming a magnet for opportunities that align with your financial goals.

Reflection Questions:

1. What financial opportunities presented themselves to you

today?

2. How did you position yourself to attract these opportunities?
3. What steps can you take to become even more open to financial opportunities?

Day 38: Affirmation for Love

Affirmation: "I radiate love, and it is reflected back to me in countless ways."

Explanation: Love is a powerful force that attracts more of itself. This affirmation reminds you that the love you give out will come back to you in various forms, enriching your life.

Reflection Questions:

1. How did you radiate love today?
2. In what ways was that love reflected back to you?
3. How can you ensure that you continue to radiate love in your daily interactions?

Day 39: Affirmation for Purpose

Affirmation: "I am fully committed to living a life of purpose and passion."

Explanation: Living with purpose and passion requires full commitment. This affirmation encourages you to dedicate yourself wholeheartedly to your purpose, ensuring that your life is vibrant and meaningful.

Reflection Questions:

1. How did you show commitment to your purpose today?
2. What passions drive you, and how do they influence your actions?
3. How can you deepen your commitment to living a purposeful life?

Day 40: Affirmation for Self-Confidence

Affirmation: "I am worthy of my dreams and capable of achieving them."

Explanation: Believing in your worth and abilities is essential for pursuing your dreams. This affirmation reinforces your self-worth and reminds you that you have the capability to achieve anything you set your mind to.

Reflection Questions:

1. How did you affirm your worthiness of your dreams today?
2. What steps did you take toward achieving your dreams?
3. How can you continue to build confidence in your ability to achieve your goals?

Day 41: Affirmation for Positivity

Affirmation: "I am grateful for the present moment and find joy in the here and now."

Explanation: Gratitude and joy are powerful tools for cultivating positivity. This affirmation encourages you to focus on the present moment, finding happiness in the here and now.

Reflection Questions:

1. What aspects of the present moment brought you joy today?
2. How did practicing gratitude enhance your positivity?
3. How can you make it a habit to find joy and gratitude in every moment?

Day 42: Affirmation for Security

Affirmation: "I trust myself to make decisions that keep me safe and secure."

Explanation: Security often comes from trusting in your own judgment and decision-making abilities. This affirmation empowers you to trust yourself, knowing that you are capable of creating a safe and secure life.

Reflection Questions:

1. How did you trust yourself in your decision-making today?
2. What decisions did you make that contributed to your

sense of security?

3. How can you continue to build trust in your ability to create a secure life?

Day 43: Affirmation for Happiness

Affirmation: "I am at peace with where I am in life, knowing that every experience is part of my journey."

Explanation: Finding peace with your current circumstances allows you to appreciate the journey, not just the destination. This affirmation encourages acceptance of where you are, understanding that every experience is valuable.

Reflection Questions:

1. How did you find peace with your current situation today?
2. What experiences have shaped your journey, and how do you value them?
3. How can you maintain a sense of peace in your life?

Day 44: Affirmation for Purpose

Affirmation: "I am making a difference in the world by living my purpose with passion."

Explanation: Living with purpose not only fulfills you but also impacts others. This affirmation reminds you that by passionately pursuing your purpose, you are making a positive difference in the world around you.

Reflection Questions:

1. How did you make a difference in someone's life today?
2. How does living your purpose benefit others?
3. What can you do to amplify your positive impact?

Day 45: Affirmation for Success

Affirmation: "I am resilient and overcome any challenges that come my way."

Explanation: Resilience is a key factor in success. This affirmation helps you build a mindset that sees challenges as opportunities for growth and reinforces your ability to overcome obstacles.

Reflection Questions:

1. What challenges did you face today, and how did you overcome them?
2. How does resilience play a role in your journey to success?
3. How can you continue to build resilience in your life?

Day 46: Affirmation for Wealth

Affirmation: "I am open to receiving unexpected sources of income."

Explanation: Wealth can come from various sources, sometimes in ways you don't anticipate. This affirmation encourages you to stay open to the possibility of receiving financial abundance in unexpected ways.

Reflection Questions:

1. How did you remain open to receiving unexpected income today?
2. What opportunities might you have overlooked that could lead to financial gain?
3. How can you stay more aware and receptive to unconventional sources of wealth?

Day 47: Affirmation for Love

Affirmation: "I give and receive love freely and effortlessly."

Explanation: Love is most powerful when it flows freely. This affirmation encourages you to remove any barriers that might prevent you from both giving and receiving love, creating an effortless exchange of affection and care.

Reflection Questions:

1. How did you give love freely today?
2. In what ways did you feel love coming back to you?

3. How can you nurture an environment where love is exchanged freely and without effort?

Day 48: Affirmation for Purpose

Affirmation: "My purpose drives me to make a positive impact in the world."

Explanation: When your purpose aligns with making a positive impact, your actions contribute to something greater than yourself. This affirmation reinforces the idea that your purpose not only benefits you but also enhances the world around you.

Reflection Questions:

1. What actions did you take today that align with your purpose and benefit others?
2. How does your purpose contribute to the greater good?
3. What can you do to amplify the positive impact of your purpose?

Day 49: Affirmation for Self-Confidence

Affirmation: "I trust in my abilities and take bold steps forward."

Explanation: Confidence comes from trusting in your own

capabilities and being willing to take risks. This affirmation encourages you to act with confidence, knowing that you have the skills and strength to succeed.

Reflection Questions:

1. What bold steps did you take today that required confidence?
2. How did trusting in your abilities influence your actions?
3. What areas of your life could benefit from more boldness and self-trust?

Day 50: Affirmation for Positivity

Affirmation: "I choose to see the good in people and situations."

Explanation: Positivity is a choice that can be made in any situation. This affirmation encourages you to consciously look for the good in others and in the circumstances you encounter, fostering a positive mindset.

Reflection Questions:

1. How did you choose to see the good in someone or something today?
2. How did this choice affect your mood and interactions?
3. How can you make it a habit to focus on the good, even in challenging situations?

Day 51: Affirmation for Security

Affirmation: "I am in control of my life and make decisions that lead to my security."

Explanation: Security often comes from feeling in control of your life and the choices you make. This affirmation empowers you to take charge of your decisions, knowing that they will lead to a more secure and stable future.

Reflection Questions:

1. What decisions did you make today that reinforced your sense of security?
2. How do you feel when you are in control of your life and choices?
3. What can you do to maintain or increase your sense of control over your life?

Day 52: Affirmation for Happiness

Affirmation: "I find joy in the present moment and appreciate the beauty around me."

Explanation: Being present allows you to fully experience the happiness and beauty of life. This affirmation encourages mindfulness and the appreciation of the simple joys that exist in the here and now.

Reflection Questions:

1. What moments today brought you joy?

2. How did being present enhance your experience of these moments?
3. How can you practice mindfulness to find more joy in your life?

Day 53: Affirmation for Purpose

Affirmation: "I am committed to living my purpose with integrity and authenticity."

Explanation: Living with integrity and authenticity is essential to fulfilling your purpose. This affirmation encourages you to stay true to yourself and your values as you pursue your goals.

Reflection Questions:

1. How did you live with integrity and authenticity today?
2. How does being true to yourself align with your purpose?
3. What challenges do you face in maintaining authenticity, and how can you overcome them?

Day 54: Affirmation for Success

Affirmation: "I am in control of my destiny and make choices that lead to success."

Explanation: Success is often the result of the choices

you make. This affirmation reinforces the idea that you have control over your destiny and encourages you to make decisions that align with your goals and aspirations.

Reflection Questions:

1. What choices did you make today that moved you closer to your goals?
2. How did you feel being in control of your decisions and actions?
3. What steps can you take to ensure your future choices continue leading you toward success?

Day 55: Affirmation for Wealth

Affirmation: "I am aligned with the energy of abundance."

Explanation: Wealth is more than just money; it's about aligning yourself with the energy of abundance in all areas of life. This affirmation helps you cultivate a mindset that attracts abundance in all its forms.

Reflection Questions:

1. How did you feel aligned with abundance today?
2. What areas of your life felt particularly abundant?
3. How can you continue to align yourself with the energy of abundance?

Day 56: Affirmation for Love

Affirmation: "I am deserving of deep, meaningful connections."

Explanation: Believing in your worthiness is key to attracting and maintaining deep, meaningful relationships. This affirmation reminds you that you are deserving of love that is profound and fulfilling.

Reflection Questions:

1. What deep, meaningful connections did you experience today?
2. How did you affirm your worthiness of such connections?
3. What can you do to nurture and sustain these meaningful relationships?

Day 57: Affirmation for Purpose

Affirmation: "I live each day with intention and purpose."

Explanation: Living with intention ensures that your actions are purposeful and aligned with your greater goals. This affirmation encourages you to approach each day with clarity and direction, making the most of every moment.

Reflection Questions:

1. How did you live with intention today?
2. What actions did you take that aligned with your purpose?
3. How can you ensure that each day is filled with purpose

and intention?

Day 58: Affirmation for Self-Confidence

Affirmation: "I am capable of achieving anything I set my mind to."

Explanation: Confidence in your ability to achieve your goals is essential for success. This affirmation reinforces your belief in your own capabilities and encourages you to pursue your dreams with determination.

Reflection Questions:

1. What goals did you pursue today with confidence?
2. How did believing in your capabilities impact your actions?
3. What can you do to continue building your confidence in achieving your goals?

Day 59: Affirmation for Positivity

Affirmation: "I attract positive experiences and opportunities into my life."

Explanation: Your mindset has a powerful influence on the experiences and opportunities that come your way. This affirmation encourages you to focus on attracting positivity,

which in turn brings more positive experiences into your life.
Reflection Questions:

1. What positive experiences or opportunities did you attract today?
2. How did your mindset influence what you attracted?
3. How can you continue to cultivate a mindset that draws positivity into your life?

Day 60: Affirmation for Security

Affirmation: "I am safe, secure, and protected at all times."

Explanation: Feeling secure comes from a deep sense of safety and protection. This affirmation reassures you that you are always safe and secure, both physically and emotionally.

Reflection Questions:

1. How did you feel safe and secure today?
2. What actions or thoughts contributed to your sense of protection?
3. How can you reinforce your feelings of safety and security on a daily basis?

Day 61: Affirmation for Happiness

Affirmation: "I am surrounded by love and support, and I cherish the relationships in my life."

Explanation: Happiness is often found in the connections you have with others. This affirmation helps you appreciate and nurture the love and support around you, recognizing the importance of healthy, positive relationships.

Reflection Questions:

1. Which relationships in your life bring you the most joy?
2. How did you show appreciation for your loved ones today?
3. How can you strengthen and nurture the connections you value?

Day 62: Affirmation for Purpose

Affirmation: "I embrace my unique path and trust that it is leading me to fulfill my purpose."

Explanation: Each person's journey is unique, and comparing yourself to others can hinder your progress. This affirmation encourages you to trust your path and believe that it is leading you exactly where you need to be.

Reflection Questions:

1. What unique aspects of your journey do you appreciate?
2. How did you trust in your path today?
3. How can you continue to embrace and trust your unique

journey?

Day 63: Affirmation for Success

Affirmation: "I attract success by being my authentic self and sharing my gifts with the world."

Explanation: Authenticity attracts opportunities and success. This affirmation encourages you to be true to yourself and share your unique gifts, knowing that success will follow when you operate from a place of authenticity.

Reflection Questions:

1. How did you express your authentic self today?
2. What gifts did you share with the world today, and how were they received?
3. How can you continue to attract success by being true to who you are?

Day 64: Affirmation for Wealth

Affirmation: "I attract wealth and prosperity with every decision I make."

Explanation: Wealth is often the result of smart, intentional decisions. This affirmation reminds you that each choice you make has the potential to bring more prosperity into your life.

Reflection Questions:

1. What decisions did you make today that align with attracting wealth?
2. How did your decisions today impact your financial outlook?
3. How can you continue making decisions that support your financial prosperity?

Day 65: Affirmation for Love

Affirmation: "I am worthy of love, and I welcome it into my life."

Explanation: Worthiness is key to receiving love. This affirmation helps you embrace the belief that you are deserving of love, which opens you up to receiving it from others.

Reflection Questions:

1. How did you affirm your worthiness of love today?
2. In what ways did love manifest in your life?
3. How can you continue to welcome love into your life with open arms?

Day 66: Affirmation for Purpose

Affirmation: "I am guided by my inner wisdom to live a purposeful life."

Explanation: Your inner wisdom is a powerful guide that can lead you toward your true purpose. This affirmation encourages you to trust your intuition and let it direct you on your path.

Reflection Questions:

1. How did your inner wisdom guide you today?
2. In what ways did you live a purposeful life?
3. How can you strengthen your connection to your inner wisdom?

Day 67: Affirmation for Self-Confidence

Affirmation: "I believe in myself and my ability to succeed."

Explanation: Belief in yourself is the foundation of self-confidence. This affirmation reinforces your faith in your abilities and encourages you to approach your goals with determination.

Reflection Questions:

1. How did your belief in yourself impact your actions today?
2. What successes did you experience as a result of your confidence?
3. How can you continue to cultivate and strengthen your

self-belief?

Day 68: Affirmation for Positivity

Affirmation: "I focus on solutions rather than problems."

Explanation: A positive mindset involves focusing on solutions rather than dwelling on problems. This affirmation encourages you to shift your focus toward finding answers and overcoming challenges.

Reflection Questions:

1. How did you focus on solutions rather than problems today?
2. What solutions did you come up with that improved your situation?
3. How can you make solution-focused thinking a regular practice?

Day 69: Affirmation for Security

Affirmation: "I am resilient and can overcome any challenge."

Explanation: Security isn't just about external circumstances; it's also about your inner strength. This affirmation reminds you of your resilience and ability to overcome any obstacles that come your way.

Reflection Questions:

1. What challenges did you face today, and how did you overcome them?
2. How did your resilience contribute to your sense of security?
3. How can you continue to build resilience in the face of future challenges?

Day 70: Affirmation for Happiness

Affirmation: "I allow myself to experience joy in all its forms and celebrate the small victories."

Explanation: Happiness can be found in both big moments and small, everyday victories. This affirmation reminds you to celebrate all forms of joy and recognize that even the smallest successes are worth acknowledging.

Reflection Questions:

1. What small victories did you celebrate today?
2. How did allowing yourself to experience joy impact your overall happiness?
3. What can you do to ensure you continue to recognize and celebrate the small wins?

Day 71: Affirmation for Purpose

Affirmation: "I am a lifelong learner, and my purpose evolves as I grow and learn."

Explanation: Purpose is not always fixed; it can evolve as you grow and gain new experiences. This affirmation encourages a mindset of continuous learning, allowing your purpose to develop and expand with you.

Reflection Questions:

1. What did you learn today that contributed to your growth?
2. How has your purpose evolved over time?
3. What steps can you take to continue learning and expanding your purpose?

Day 72: Affirmation for Success

Affirmation: "I am proactive and take inspired action towards my goals."

Explanation: Success often requires taking initiative and acting on your inspirations. This affirmation encourages you to be proactive in pursuing your goals, taking deliberate steps that are aligned with your vision for success.

Reflection Questions:

1. What inspired actions did you take today towards your goals?
2. How did being proactive make a difference in your

progress?

3. What more can you do to ensure consistent, inspired action?

Day 73: Affirmation for Wealth

Affirmation: "I am worthy of financial success and abundance."

Explanation: Recognizing your worth is the first step toward achieving financial success. This affirmation helps you internalize the belief that you deserve to be financially successful, opening the door to greater abundance in your life.

Reflection Questions:

1. In what ways did you acknowledge your worthiness of financial success today?
2. How has believing in your financial worth influenced your decisions?
3. What steps can you take to continue embracing your financial worthiness?

Day 74: Affirmation for Love

Affirmation: "I attract healthy, loving relationships into my life."

Explanation: Healthy relationships are built on mutual respect, trust, and love. This affirmation sets the intention to attract relationships that are nurturing, supportive, and filled with positive energy.

Reflection Questions:

1. What qualities do you value in a healthy, loving relationship?
2. How did you attract or nurture such relationships today?
3. What boundaries or standards do you need to uphold to ensure your relationships remain healthy?

Day 75: Affirmation for Purpose

Affirmation: "Every day, I am getting closer to my life's true purpose."

Explanation: Purpose is a journey, not a destination. This affirmation reassures you that with each passing day, you are making progress toward discovering and fulfilling your life's purpose.

Reflection Questions:

1. What actions did you take today that align with your life's purpose?

2. How do you feel about your progress toward your purpose?
3. What small steps can you take tomorrow to continue moving closer to your true purpose?

Day 76: Affirmation for Self-Confidence

Affirmation: "I am proud of who I am and what I have achieved."

Explanation: Self-confidence often comes from acknowledging your achievements and taking pride in who you are. This affirmation helps you recognize your worth and build confidence by celebrating your successes.

Reflection Questions:

1. What achievements are you proud of today?
2. How did acknowledging your achievements affect your self-confidence?
3. How can you make it a habit to celebrate your successes, both big and small?

Day 77: Affirmation for Positivity

Affirmation: "I choose to radiate positivity in every situation."

Explanation: Positivity is a choice that you can make in any circumstance. This affirmation encourages you to consciously radiate positive energy, which can uplift both yourself and those around you.

Reflection Questions:

1. How did you choose to radiate positivity today?
2. What impact did your positive energy have on your environment?
3. How can you maintain a positive outlook even in challenging situations?

Day 78: Affirmation for Security

Affirmation: "I am surrounded by a safe and supportive environment."

Explanation: Security is enhanced when you feel safe and supported by your surroundings. This affirmation helps you recognize and appreciate the safety and support you have in your life.

Reflection Questions:

1. In what ways did you feel supported and safe today?
2. How does your environment contribute to your sense of security?

3. What can you do to strengthen the safety and support in your surroundings?

Day 79: Affirmation for Happiness

Affirmation: "I am deserving of happiness, and I welcome it into my life with open arms."

Explanation: Believing that you deserve happiness is crucial to actually experiencing it. This affirmation reinforces your self-worth and invites more happiness into your life by affirming that you are deserving of it.

Reflection Questions:

1. How did you welcome happiness into your life today?
2. What beliefs about your self-worth might be affecting your happiness?
3. How can you continue to affirm your deservingness of joy and happiness?

Day 80: Affirmation for Purpose

Affirmation: "I align my actions with my values and purpose, creating a life of meaning."

Explanation: Living a purposeful life means aligning your actions with your core values. This affirmation encourages you to be intentional with your actions, ensuring they reflect your values and contribute to a meaningful life.

Reflection Questions:

1. What actions did you take today that aligned with your values?
2. How do these actions contribute to your sense of purpose?
3. Are there areas in your life where you need to realign your actions with your values?

Day 81: Affirmation for Success

Affirmation: "I turn challenges into opportunities for growth and success."

Explanation: Challenges are inevitable, but they can also be opportunities for growth. This affirmation encourages you to see obstacles as stepping stones to success, fostering a mindset that turns difficulties into advantages.

Reflection Questions:

1. What challenges did you face today, and how did you turn them into opportunities?
2. How has overcoming challenges in the past contributed to your success?
3. What can you do to maintain a positive mindset when facing future challenges?

Day 82: Affirmation for Wealth

Affirmation: "I am a magnet for financial opportunities and prosperity."

Explanation: Wealth often comes from being open to and attracting financial opportunities. This affirmation positions you as a magnet for prosperity, encouraging you to remain receptive to the financial abundance that is available.

Reflection Questions:

1. What financial opportunities did you attract today?
2. How did being open to prosperity influence your actions?
3. How can you stay alert to new financial opportunities in the future?

Day 83: Affirmation for Love

Affirmation: "My heart is open to giving and receiving love."

Explanation: An open heart is essential for both giving and receiving love. This affirmation encourages you to keep your heart open, fostering deeper connections and greater love in your life.

Reflection Questions:

1. How did you give and receive love today?
2. What did having an open heart bring into your life?
3. How can you continue to cultivate an open-hearted approach to your relationships?

Day 84: Affirmation for Purpose

Affirmation: "I trust that I am exactly where I need to be in my journey."

Explanation: Trusting the process is key to fulfilling your purpose. This affirmation reminds you that you are on the right path, even if it doesn't always feel that way, and that each step is part of your journey.

Reflection Questions:

1. How did you trust the process of your journey today?
2. What signs or experiences reassured you that you are on the right path?
3. How can you strengthen your trust in the journey toward your purpose?

Day 85: Affirmation for Self-Confidence

Affirmation: "I embrace my uniqueness and let it shine."

Explanation: Confidence grows when you fully embrace and celebrate what makes you unique. This affirmation encourages you to take pride in your individuality and to let your unique qualities shine through.

Reflection Questions:

1. What unique qualities did you embrace today?
2. How did embracing your uniqueness boost your confidence?

3. How can you continue to let your individuality shine in your daily life?

Day 86: Affirmation for Positivity

Affirmation: "I choose thoughts that nourish and uplift my spirit."

Explanation: Positive thoughts are essential for maintaining a positive mindset. This affirmation encourages you to consciously choose thoughts that nourish your spirit and keep you uplifted.

Reflection Questions:

1. What uplifting thoughts did you focus on today?
2. How did these thoughts affect your mood and actions?
3. How can you make it a habit to choose nourishing thoughts throughout the day?

Day 87: Affirmation for Security

Affirmation: "I am grounded, centered, and secure in who I am."

Explanation: True security comes from being grounded and centered in your sense of self. This affirmation reinforces your inner stability, helping you feel secure in who you are, no matter what life brings.

Reflection Questions:

1. How did you feel grounded and centered today?
2. In what ways did this sense of inner security influence your actions?
3. What practices can you incorporate to maintain a strong sense of self-security?

Day 88: Affirmation for Happiness

Affirmation: "I am the architect of my happiness, and I design a life filled with joy."

Explanation: You have the power to create your own happiness. This affirmation reminds you that your choices, thoughts, and actions all contribute to building a life that is joyful and fulfilling.

Reflection Questions:

1. How did you design your happiness today?
2. What choices contributed to your sense of joy?
3. How can you continue to be intentional in creating a joyful life?

Day 89: Affirmation for Purpose

Affirmation: "I am driven by a deep sense of purpose that guides me through life's journey."

Explanation: A strong sense of purpose provides direction and motivation. This affirmation reinforces your connection to your purpose, serving as a guiding force that helps you navigate life's journey with intention.

Reflection Questions:

1. How did your sense of purpose guide you today?
2. What actions did you take that were driven by your purpose?
3. How can you deepen your connection to your purpose?

Day 90: Affirmation for Success

Affirmation: "I celebrate my successes, big and small, and use them as motivation for future achievements."

Explanation: Celebrating your successes, no matter the size, reinforces positive behavior and motivates you to continue striving for more. This affirmation encourages you to acknowledge and appreciate your achievements as fuel for future success.

Reflection Questions:

1. What successes did you celebrate today?
2. How did celebrating these achievements motivate you for

the future?

3. How can you create a habit of celebrating your successes regularly?

Day 91: Affirmation for Wealth

Affirmation: "I am grateful for the wealth I have and the wealth that is coming."

Explanation: Gratitude is a powerful tool for attracting more of what you want, including wealth. This affirmation helps you express gratitude for your current financial situation while also welcoming future abundance.

Reflection Questions:

1. What aspects of your current financial situation are you grateful for?
2. How did expressing gratitude influence your outlook on wealth?
3. How can you maintain a mindset of gratitude for both present and future wealth?

Day 92: Affirmation for Love

Affirmation: "I am surrounded by love, kindness, and compassion."

Explanation: Love thrives in an environment filled with

kindness and compassion. This affirmation helps you recognize and attract these qualities in your relationships, creating a loving and supportive atmosphere.

Reflection Questions:

1. How did you experience love, kindness, and compassion today?
2. What impact did these qualities have on your relationships?
3. How can you continue to foster an environment of love and compassion?

Day 93: Affirmation for Purpose

Affirmation: "My purpose is unfolding before me with clarity and grace."

Explanation: Discovering your purpose is often a gradual process. This affirmation reassures you that your purpose is becoming clearer with time, and that you are on a path of grace and understanding.

Reflection Questions:

1. How did you gain clarity on your purpose today?
2. What moments of grace did you experience as your purpose unfolded?
3. How can you continue to trust the process as your purpose becomes clearer?

Day 94: Affirmation for Self-Confidence

Affirmation: "I am worthy of respect and appreciation."

Explanation: Confidence is bolstered by recognizing your own worthiness. This affirmation reminds you that you deserve to be respected and appreciated, just as you are.

Reflection Questions:

1. In what ways did you feel respected and appreciated today?
2. How did acknowledging your worthiness impact your self-confidence?
3. What actions can you take to ensure that you are treated with the respect and appreciation you deserve?

Day 95: Affirmation for Positivity

Affirmation: "I find joy in the simple moments of life."

Explanation: Positivity often comes from appreciating the small, simple moments that bring joy. This affirmation encourages you to focus on the little things that make life beautiful, enhancing your overall sense of happiness.

Reflection Questions:

1. What simple moments brought you joy today?
2. How did focusing on these moments affect your overall positivity?
3. How can you make it a habit to find joy in the simple

things every day?

Day 96: Affirmation for Security

Affirmation: "I trust in the process of life and know I am protected."

Explanation: Trusting the process of life contributes to a deep sense of security. This affirmation helps you feel protected and safe, knowing that everything is unfolding as it should.

Reflection Questions:

1. How did you trust the process of life today?
2. In what ways did you feel protected and secure?
3. What can you do to deepen your trust in life's unfolding journey?

Day 97: Affirmation for Wealth

Affirmation: "I am worthy of a wealthy and fulfilling life."

Explanation: Wealth is not just about financial prosperity but also about a fulfilling life filled with purpose and joy. This affirmation reinforces the belief that you deserve both financial abundance and a life that is rich in experiences and meaning.

Reflection Questions:

1. How did you embrace your worthiness of a wealthy and fulfilling life today?
2. What steps did you take to enhance both your financial wealth and personal fulfillment?
3. How can you continue to cultivate a mindset that values both material wealth and meaningful life experiences?

Day 98: Affirmation for Love

Affirmation: "Love flows to me and through me effortlessly."

Explanation: Love is both given and received effortlessly when you are open to it. This affirmation encourages you to see love as an abundant, flowing energy that you can both give and receive with ease.

Reflection Questions:

1. How did you experience love flowing to and through you today?
2. What actions did you take to allow love to flow more freely in your life?
3. How can you continue to nurture the effortless flow of love in your relationships?

Day 99: Affirmation for Purpose

Affirmation: "I am aligned with my true purpose and guided by my inner wisdom."

Explanation: Aligning with your true purpose means listening to and trusting your inner wisdom. This affirmation reinforces the belief that you are on the right path and that your inner guidance will lead you toward fulfilling your purpose.

Reflection Questions:

1. How did you feel aligned with your purpose today?
2. What role did your inner wisdom play in guiding your actions?
3. How can you strengthen your connection to your inner wisdom to stay aligned with your purpose?

Day 100: Affirmation for Self-Confidence

Affirmation: "I believe in myself and my abilities."

Explanation: Self-confidence stems from a strong belief in your own abilities. This affirmation helps you internalize the confidence needed to tackle challenges and pursue your goals with conviction.

Reflection Questions:

1. How did you demonstrate belief in yourself and your abilities today?
2. In what ways did this belief influence your actions and

decisions?

3. What can you do to reinforce your self-belief and confidence moving forward?

Day 101: Affirmation for Positivity

Affirmation: "I choose to see the good in every situation."

Explanation: Positivity is about finding the silver lining in all circumstances. This affirmation encourages you to focus on the good, even in challenging situations, which can help maintain a positive outlook.

Reflection Questions:

1. What positive aspects did you find in today's situations?
2. How did choosing to see the good impact your mood and interactions?
3. How can you continue to train your mind to focus on the positive, even in difficult times?

Day 102: Affirmation for Security

Affirmation: "I am secure in the knowledge that all my needs are met."

Explanation: Security comes from trusting that your needs, both material and emotional, will always be met. This affirmation reassures you that you are cared for and that you can rely on the universe to provide for you.

Reflection Questions:

1. How did you feel secure in knowing that your needs were met today?
2. In what ways did this sense of security influence your actions or decisions?
3. How can you continue to cultivate a mindset of trust in the provision of your needs?

Day 103: Affirmation for Wealth

Affirmation: "My financial success is a reflection of my inner growth."

Explanation: True wealth often mirrors your inner growth and development. This affirmation connects your financial success to your personal evolution, encouraging you to focus on inner growth as a path to greater wealth.

Reflection Questions:

1. How did your financial success today reflect your personal growth?
2. What inner qualities have contributed most to your financial achievements?
3. How can you continue to grow internally to expand your financial success?

Day 104: Affirmation for Love

Affirmation: "I am deserving of love and happiness in all forms."

Explanation: Everyone deserves love and happiness, no matter their circumstances. This affirmation helps you internalize the belief that you are inherently deserving of all forms of love and joy.

Reflection Questions:

1. How did you experience love and happiness today?
2. In what ways did you affirm your deservingness of these feelings?
3. How can you continue to embrace and welcome love and happiness into your life?

Day 105: Affirmation for Purpose

Affirmation: "I am a powerful creator of my destiny."

Explanation: You have the power to shape your future and fulfill your purpose. This affirmation empowers you to take control of your life and actively create the destiny you desire.

Reflection Questions:

1. What actions did you take today to create your desired destiny?
2. How did recognizing your power as a creator influence your decisions?

3. How can you continue to harness your creative power to fulfill your purpose?

Day 106: Affirmation for Self-Confidence

Affirmation: "I am confident in the face of challenges and rise above them."

Explanation: Confidence is crucial when facing challenges. This affirmation reminds you that you have the strength and ability to overcome obstacles, boosting your resilience and self-assurance.

Reflection Questions:

1. What challenges did you face today, and how did you approach them with confidence?
2. How did your confidence help you rise above difficulties?
3. What strategies can you use to maintain your confidence in the face of future challenges?

Day 107: Affirmation for Positivity

Affirmation: "I am a beacon of light and positivity for myself and others."

Explanation: Positivity not only uplifts you but also those around you. This affirmation encourages you to be a source of light, spreading positive energy in your life and in the lives of others.

Reflection Questions:

1. How did you serve as a beacon of positivity today?
2. What impact did your positive energy have on yourself and others?
3. How can you continue to shine light and positivity in your daily interactions?

Day 108: Affirmation for Security

Affirmation: "I am safe, supported, and secure in every aspect of my life."

Explanation: Feeling secure comes from knowing you are safe and supported in all areas of life. This affirmation reinforces your sense of security, helping you feel grounded and protected.

Reflection Questions:

1. In what ways did you feel safe and supported today?
2. How did this sense of security influence your overall well-being?
3. What steps can you take to further enhance your sense of safety and support?

Day 109: Affirmation for Wealth

Affirmation: "I am open to receiving unexpected sources of income."

Explanation: Sometimes wealth comes from unexpected places. This affirmation encourages you to remain open and receptive to all forms of financial abundance, even those that come from surprising sources.

Reflection Questions:

1. Did you receive any unexpected income or opportunities today?
2. How did being open to unexpected abundance affect your mindset?
3. How can you maintain an open and receptive attitude toward new sources of wealth?

Day 110: Affirmation for Love

Affirmation: "I give and receive love freely and without fear."

Explanation: Love should be given and received without fear or hesitation. This affirmation encourages you to embrace love fully, letting go of any fears that may hold you back from deeper connections.

Reflection Questions:

1. How did you give and receive love freely today?
2. What fears, if any, did you overcome to fully embrace

love?

3. How can you continue to let go of fear and allow love to flow freely in your life?

Day 111: Affirmation for Purpose

Affirmation: "I am on the path to fulfilling my highest potential."

Explanation: Your purpose is tied to reaching your highest potential. This affirmation reassures you that you are on the right path and encourages you to strive for the best version of yourself.

Reflection Questions:

1. How did you work toward fulfilling your highest potential today?
2. What steps did you take that aligned with your purpose?
3. How can you continue to move forward on the path to achieving your full potential?

Day 112: Affirmation for Self-Confidence

Affirmation: "I trust myself to make the right decisions."

Explanation: Confidence in your decision-making abilities is crucial for self-assurance. This affirmation strengthens your trust in your judgment, helping you feel more secure in the choices you make.

Reflection Questions:

1. What decisions did you make today, and how did you trust yourself in the process?
2. How did trusting your decision-making abilities affect the outcome?
3. What can you do to continue building trust in your own judgment?

Day 113: Affirmation for Positivity

Affirmation: "I choose to focus on the bright side of life."

Explanation: Positivity is often about where you choose to focus your attention. This affirmation encourages you to look on the bright side, cultivating a mindset that emphasizes the good in every situation.

Reflection Questions:

1. What bright sides did you focus on today?
2. How did this focus influence your mood and actions?
3. How can you train your mind to consistently look for the positive aspects of life?

Day 114: Affirmation for Security

Affirmation: "I am deeply rooted in my sense of self and security."

Explanation: Security is strengthened by a strong sense of self. This affirmation helps you feel grounded and stable in who you are, enhancing your overall sense of security.

Reflection Questions:

1. How did you feel rooted in your sense of self and security today?
2. What actions or thoughts contributed to this deep sense of security?
3. How can you continue to cultivate and strengthen your sense of self to maintain this security?

Day 115: Affirmation for Wealth

Affirmation: "I attract opportunities that lead to financial growth and prosperity."

Explanation: Wealth often comes through the opportunities you attract. This affirmation opens your mind to the possibilities of financial growth by acknowledging that you are a magnet for prosperity-enhancing opportunities.

Reflection Questions:

1. What opportunities for financial growth did you encounter today?

2. How did your mindset help you attract these opportunities?
3. How can you remain open to new opportunities that lead to greater wealth and prosperity?

Day 116: Affirmation for Love

Affirmation: "I am surrounded by love, and I radiate love to others."

Explanation: Love is both received and given in abundance. This affirmation helps you recognize the love that surrounds you and encourages you to share that love with others, creating a cycle of positivity and connection.

Reflection Questions:

1. How did you feel surrounded by love today?
2. In what ways did you radiate love to others?
3. How can you continue to foster an environment where love is both received and given freely?

Day 117: Affirmation for Purpose

Affirmation: "Every day, I move closer to living my true purpose."

Explanation: Purpose is a journey, not a destination. This affirmation reminds you that every step you take is bringing you closer to living a life that is aligned with your true purpose.

Reflection Questions:

1. What steps did you take today that brought you closer to your true purpose?
2. How did your actions align with your sense of purpose?
3. How can you ensure that each day, you continue to move closer to fully living your purpose?

Day 118: Affirmation for Self-Confidence

Affirmation: "I am confident in my uniqueness and embrace what makes me different."

Explanation: Self-confidence is rooted in embracing your uniqueness. This affirmation encourages you to celebrate what makes you different, recognizing that your individuality is a source of strength.

Reflection Questions:

1. How did you embrace your uniqueness today?
2. In what ways did your confidence in your individuality influence your actions?
3. How can you continue to celebrate and embrace what makes you different?

Day 119: Affirmation for Positivity

Affirmation: "I attract positive energy and release all negativity."

Explanation: Positivity is about the energy you attract and the negativity you release. This affirmation helps you focus on drawing in positive energy while letting go of anything that does not serve you.

Reflection Questions:

1. What positive energy did you attract today?
2. How did you release negativity that was holding you back?
3. How can you continue to attract positivity and release negativity in your life?

Day 120: Affirmation for Security

Affirmation: "I am confident in my ability to create a secure future."

Explanation: Security in life is often a result of confidence in your ability to shape your future. This affirmation reinforces your belief that you have the power and the tools to create the security you desire.

Reflection Questions:

1. How did you demonstrate confidence in your ability to create security today?
2. What steps did you take to ensure a secure future?

3. How can you continue to build and maintain confidence in your ability to create security?

Day 121: Affirmation for Wealth

Affirmation: "My actions align with my goals for financial abundance."

Explanation: Wealth is a result of actions that align with your financial goals. This affirmation helps you stay focused on making decisions that lead to financial abundance, ensuring that your daily choices support your long-term wealth.

Reflection Questions:

1. How did your actions today align with your financial goals?
2. In what ways did your decisions contribute to your financial abundance?
3. How can you continue to align your actions with your goals for greater wealth?

Day 122: Affirmation for Love

Affirmation: "I am a magnet for loving and nurturing relationships."

Explanation: The relationships you attract reflect the energy you put out. This affirmation helps you draw in relationships that are loving, supportive, and nurturing, fostering a strong network of positive connections.

Reflection Questions:

1. What loving and nurturing relationships did you experience today?
2. How did you contribute to the positivity and strength of your relationships?
3. How can you continue to attract and nurture relationships that are supportive and loving?

Day 123: Affirmation for Purpose

Affirmation: "I am driven by a clear sense of purpose and direction."

Explanation: A clear sense of purpose gives you direction and motivation. This affirmation reminds you that knowing your purpose fuels your drive, helping you stay focused and intentional in your actions.

Reflection Questions:

1. How did your sense of purpose drive your actions today?
2. What steps did you take to stay aligned with your direction and goals?
3. How can you maintain clarity and focus on your purpose in the days ahead?

Day 124: Affirmation for Self-Confidence

Affirmation: "I trust in my abilities to achieve my dreams."

Explanation: Confidence in your abilities is key to achieving your dreams. This affirmation reinforces your belief in yourself, empowering you to take the necessary steps toward making your dreams a reality.

Reflection Questions:

1. How did you demonstrate trust in your abilities today?
2. What actions did you take that moved you closer to achieving your dreams?
3. How can you continue to build confidence in your abilities to reach your goals?

Day 125: Affirmation for Positivity

Affirmation: "I am grateful for all the positivity in my life."

Explanation: Gratitude amplifies positivity. This affirmation helps you recognize and appreciate all the positive aspects of your life, fostering a mindset of abundance and joy.

Reflection Questions:

1. What positive aspects of your life were you most grateful for today?
2. How did focusing on gratitude enhance your overall positivity?
3. How can you continue to cultivate a sense of gratitude to

maintain a positive outlook?

Day 126: Affirmation for Security

Affirmation: "I am surrounded by stability and security in all areas of my life."

Explanation: Security is about feeling stable and supported in every area of your life. This affirmation encourages you to recognize and build on the stability you already have, reinforcing your sense of security.

Reflection Questions:

1. In what areas of your life did you feel most stable and secure today?
2. How did this sense of stability influence your actions and decisions?
3. How can you continue to create and maintain stability and security in your life?

Day 127: Affirmation for Wealth

Affirmation: "I am capable of generating unlimited income through my skills and talents."

Explanation: Your skills and talents are valuable assets that can generate wealth. This affirmation reminds you of your potential to create unlimited income by leveraging what you are good at.

Reflection Questions:

1. How did you use your skills and talents to generate income today?
2. What steps did you take to maximize your potential for earning?
3. How can you continue to develop and leverage your skills for greater financial success?

Day 128: Affirmation for Love

Affirmation: "I am open to receiving and giving love without conditions."

Explanation: Unconditional love is the purest form of love. This affirmation encourages you to both give and receive love without any conditions or expectations, fostering deeper and more genuine connections.

Reflection Questions:

1. How did you experience unconditional love today?
2. In what ways did you give love without expecting anything in return?
3. How can you continue to nurture a mindset of unconditional love in your relationships?

Day 129: Affirmation for Purpose

Affirmation: "My life is a reflection of my true purpose and passion."

Explanation: When you live in alignment with your purpose and passion, your life reflects it in every way. This affirmation helps you stay connected to what truly drives you, ensuring that your life is a manifestation of your deepest values and desires.

Reflection Questions:

1. How did your actions today reflect your true purpose and passion?
2. What steps did you take to align your life more closely with your purpose?
3. How can you continue to ensure that your life is a true reflection of your passion and purpose?

Day 130: Affirmation for Self-Confidence

Affirmation: "I am proud of who I am and all I have accomplished."

Explanation: Self-confidence comes from pride in who you are and what you've achieved. This affirmation encourages you to recognize and celebrate your accomplishments, boosting your self-esteem and confidence.

Reflection Questions:

1. What accomplishments are you most proud of today?
2. How did acknowledging your achievements enhance your self-confidence?
3. How can you continue to celebrate your successes and build confidence in yourself?

Day 131: Affirmation for Positivity

Affirmation: "I am a positive force in the world, spreading joy and kindness."

Explanation: Positivity has a ripple effect, spreading to those around you. This affirmation encourages you to be a source of joy and kindness, making a positive impact on the world.

Reflection Questions:

1. How did you spread joy and kindness today?
2. What impact did your positive actions have on others?
3. How can you continue to be a positive force in the lives of those around you?

Day 132: Affirmation for Security

Affirmation: "I trust that everything I need to feel secure is already within me."

Explanation: True security comes from within, not from external sources. This affirmation reminds you that you possess all the inner strength, resources, and resilience needed to create and maintain a secure life.

Reflection Questions:

1. How did you draw on your inner resources to feel secure today?
2. What moments made you realize that security is something you create from within?
3. How can you continue to trust in your inner strength to feel secure in all situations?

Day 133: Affirmation for Wealth

Affirmation: "I am constantly attracting wealth and abundance into my life."

Explanation: This affirmation emphasizes the idea that wealth and abundance are naturally drawn to you. By believing that you are a magnet for prosperity, you open yourself up to new opportunities and financial growth.

Reflection Questions:

1. What signs of wealth and abundance did you notice in

your life today?

2. How did your actions contribute to attracting more prosperity?
3. How can you maintain a mindset that continuously attracts wealth and abundance?

Day 134: Affirmation for Love

Affirmation: "My heart is open, and I am ready to welcome new love into my life."

Explanation: An open heart is key to receiving love. This affirmation encourages you to remain open and receptive to love, whether it's a new romantic relationship or deeper connections with friends and family.

Reflection Questions:

1. How did you keep your heart open to love today?
2. What new or deepened connections did you experience?
3. How can you continue to welcome love into your life with an open heart?

Day 135: Affirmation for Purpose

Affirmation: "I am committed to living a life filled with purpose and meaning."

Explanation: Commitment to your purpose ensures that your life is meaningful. This affirmation reinforces your dedication to living in alignment with what truly matters to you.

Reflection Questions:

1. How did your actions today reflect your commitment to purpose and meaning?
2. What steps did you take to ensure that your life is aligned with your values?
3. How can you strengthen your commitment to living a purposeful life?

Day 136: Affirmation for Self-Confidence

Affirmation: "I believe in myself and my ability to succeed."

Explanation: Self-confidence is rooted in belief. This affirmation encourages you to trust in your abilities and potential, reinforcing the belief that you can succeed in whatever you set out to do.

Reflection Questions:

1. How did you demonstrate belief in yourself today?
2. What successes did you achieve that reinforced your self-

confidence?

3. How can you continue to build belief in your ability to succeed?

Day 137: Affirmation for Positivity

Affirmation: "I choose to focus on the good in every situation."

Explanation: Positivity is a choice. This affirmation helps you consciously decide to focus on the positive aspects of any situation, which can improve your overall outlook and well-being.

Reflection Questions:

1. What positive aspects did you focus on today, even in challenging situations?
2. How did this choice affect your mood and interactions?
3. How can you continue to focus on the good, no matter the circumstances?

Day 138: Affirmation for Security

Affirmation: "I am creating a foundation of stability and security in my life."

Explanation: Security is often about the foundation you build. This affirmation helps you focus on creating and maintaining a stable and secure base for all aspects of your life, from finances to relationships.

Reflection Questions:

1. What actions did you take today to strengthen your foundation of stability?
2. How did your choices contribute to a greater sense of security?
3. How can you continue to build a strong, secure foundation in your life?

Day 139: Affirmation for Wealth

Affirmation: "My financial success is a reflection of my hard work and dedication."

Explanation: Wealth is often the result of effort and persistence. This affirmation reminds you that your financial success is a direct outcome of your hard work, encouraging you to stay dedicated to your goals.

Reflection Questions:

1. How did your hard work contribute to financial success today?
2. In what ways can you see your dedication paying off in terms of wealth?
3. How can you continue to work hard and stay dedicated to your financial goals?

Day 140: Affirmation for Love

Affirmation: "I deserve love that is kind, genuine, and unconditional."

Explanation: Everyone deserves love that is pure and true. This affirmation helps you recognize your worth and attract relationships that are based on kindness, authenticity, and unconditional support.

Reflection Questions:

1. How did you experience kind and genuine love today?
2. What steps did you take to ensure that your relationships are rooted in unconditional love?
3. How can you continue to attract and nurture love that is deserving of you?

Day 141: Affirmation for Purpose

Affirmation: "I am living my life with clear intention and purpose."

Explanation: Clarity of intention aligns your actions with your purpose. This affirmation encourages you to live with a clear sense of direction, ensuring that everything you do is purposeful and meaningful.

Reflection Questions:

1. How did you demonstrate clear intention in your actions today?

2. What purpose guided your decisions and behaviors?
3. How can you maintain clarity of intention in your daily life?

Day 142: Affirmation for Self-Confidence

Affirmation: "I trust myself to make the right decisions."

Explanation: Self-confidence often stems from trusting your judgment. This affirmation reinforces your belief in your ability to make the best decisions for yourself, fostering a deeper sense of self-assurance.

Reflection Questions:

1. What decisions did you make today that required trust in your judgment?
2. How did these decisions impact your confidence?
3. How can you continue to trust yourself to make the right choices in the future?

Day 143: Affirmation for Positivity

Affirmation: "I attract positive outcomes through my optimistic mindset."

Explanation: A positive mindset attracts positive outcomes. This affirmation encourages you to maintain optimism, which in turn helps to create a reality filled with positive experiences and results.

Reflection Questions:

1. What positive outcomes did you attract today with your optimistic mindset?
2. How did your positivity influence the events and interactions in your day?
3. How can you continue to use optimism to attract positive results in your life?

Day 144: Affirmation for Security

Affirmation: "I am safe, supported, and secure in all that I do."

Explanation: Feeling safe and supported is crucial for a sense of security. This affirmation helps you acknowledge the safety and support that surrounds you, reinforcing your feeling of security in all aspects of life.

Reflection Questions:

1. How did you feel safe and supported today?
2. What actions or thoughts contributed to your sense of security?
3. How can you continue to cultivate an environment of safety and support?

Day 145: Affirmation for Wealth

Affirmation: "I am open to receiving abundance in all its forms."

Explanation: Wealth and abundance can come in many forms, not just financial. This affirmation encourages you to remain open to receiving all types of abundance, from money to opportunities to love.

Reflection Questions:

1. What forms of abundance did you receive today?
2. How did staying open to abundance enhance your life?
3. How can you continue to be open to the many forms of abundance that come your way?

Day 146: Affirmation for Love

Affirmation: "I give and receive love freely and joyfully."

Explanation: Love is most powerful when it flows freely. This affirmation encourages you to give and receive love without hesitation or restriction, enhancing your relationships and overall sense of joy.

Reflection Questions:

1. How did you freely give and receive love today?
2. What joy did this flow of love bring into your life?
3. How can you continue to nurture an environment where love is exchanged openly and joyfully?

Day 147: Affirmation for Purpose

Affirmation: "My purpose is unfolding perfectly in its own time."

Explanation: Purpose doesn't always reveal itself immediately. This affirmation reminds you to trust the timing of your life's purpose, knowing that it will unfold exactly as it's meant to.

Reflection Questions:

1. What signs did you notice today that your purpose is unfolding?
2. How did trusting the timing of your purpose impact your actions?
3. How can you continue to have patience as your purpose unfolds?

Day 148: Affirmation for Self-Confidence

Affirmation: "I am worthy of all the good things that come my way."

Explanation: Recognizing your worth is key to building self-confidence. This affirmation helps you affirm that you are deserving of all the good things that life has to offer, boosting your sense of self-worth.

Reflection Questions:

1. What good things did you receive today that reminded

you of your worth?

2. How did acknowledging your worth affect your confidence?
3. How can you continue to affirm your worthiness of good things in life?

Day 149: Affirmation for Positivity

Affirmation: "I see the beauty and goodness in every situation."

Explanation: Finding beauty and goodness, even in difficult situations, is a powerful way to maintain positivity. This affirmation helps you focus on the positive aspects of life, no matter what challenges arise.

Reflection Questions:

1. What beauty and goodness did you find in today's situations?
2. How did this focus on positivity affect your mood and interactions?
3. How can you consistently find beauty and goodness, even in challenging times?

Day 150: Affirmation for Security

Affirmation: "I am grounded and stable, no matter what life brings."

Explanation: Feeling grounded and stable is crucial for a sense of security. This affirmation helps you maintain your composure and confidence, regardless of external circumstances.

Reflection Questions:

1. How did you stay grounded and stable today?
2. What challenges tested your sense of security, and how did you respond?
3. How can you strengthen your ability to remain grounded in the face of uncertainty?

Day 151: Affirmation for Wealth

Affirmation: "I am grateful for the abundance that flows into my life."

Explanation: Gratitude enhances your awareness of the abundance already present in your life. This affirmation encourages you to recognize and appreciate the wealth you have, attracting even more prosperity.

Reflection Questions:

1. What aspects of your life are you grateful for today?
2. How did expressing gratitude affect your perception of

abundance?

3. How can you make gratitude a regular practice to attract more wealth?

Day 152: Affirmation for Love

Affirmation: "I am surrounded by loving and supportive relationships."

Explanation: Acknowledging the love and support you receive reinforces positive relationships. This affirmation helps you appreciate the people who care about you and foster deeper connections.

Reflection Questions:

1. Who showed you love and support today?
2. How did these relationships enhance your sense of well-being?
3. How can you nurture and strengthen your supportive relationships?

Day 153: Affirmation for Purpose

Affirmation: "Every step I take brings me closer to fulfilling my purpose."

Explanation: Progress toward your purpose is made through consistent action. This affirmation reinforces the idea that each action, no matter how small, brings you closer to your ultimate goal.

Reflection Questions:

1. What steps did you take today toward fulfilling your purpose?
2. How did these actions contribute to your sense of progress?
3. How can you maintain momentum as you continue to work towards your purpose?

Day 154: Affirmation for Self-Confidence

Affirmation: "I am proud of who I am and the journey I am on."

Explanation: Self-confidence grows from self-acceptance and pride in your journey. This affirmation helps you appreciate your progress and the person you are becoming.

Reflection Questions:

1. What aspects of yourself and your journey are you most proud of today?
2. How did this pride influence your self-confidence?
3. How can you regularly acknowledge and celebrate your achievements?

Day 155: Affirmation for Positivity

Affirmation: "I choose to see challenges as opportunities for growth."

Explanation: Viewing challenges as opportunities transforms obstacles into learning experiences. This affirmation encourages a positive outlook by recognizing the potential for growth in every difficulty.

Reflection Questions:

1. What challenges did you face today, and how did you view them?
2. How did this perspective impact your approach to solving problems?
3. How can you apply this mindset to future challenges to foster growth?

Day 156: Affirmation for Security

Affirmation: "I am resilient and capable of handling any situation."

Explanation: Resilience is key to feeling secure. This affirmation helps you build confidence in your ability to handle various situations, reinforcing your sense of security.

Reflection Questions:

1. How did your resilience help you navigate today's situations?

2. What strengths did you draw upon to handle challenges?
3. How can you continue to build resilience in your daily life?

Day 157: Affirmation for Wealth

Affirmation: "I am worthy of financial success and abundance."

Explanation: Believing in your worthiness is essential for attracting financial success. This affirmation reinforces your deservingness of prosperity and encourages a positive attitude toward wealth.

Reflection Questions:

1. How did you affirm your worthiness of financial success today?
2. What actions or thoughts reinforced this belief?
3. How can you continue to embrace your worthiness of abundance?

Day 158: Affirmation for Love

Affirmation: "I am deserving of love that enriches my life."

Explanation: Recognizing your worthiness of enriching love helps you attract and maintain meaningful relationships. This affirmation encourages you to seek out and appreciate love that adds value to your life.

Reflection Questions:

1. How did you experience enriching love today?
2. In what ways did this love add value to your life?
3. How can you continue to seek and nurture love that enhances your well-being?

Day 159: Affirmation for Purpose

Affirmation: "My actions align with my deepest values and goals."

Explanation: Alignment between your actions and values ensures that you are living purposefully. This affirmation helps you stay focused on goals that reflect your true self.

Reflection Questions:

1. How did your actions today align with your values and goals?
2. What impact did this alignment have on your sense of purpose?
3. How can you ensure that your future actions remain aligned with your values?

Day 160: Affirmation for Self-Confidence

Affirmation: "I am confident in my abilities and trust my instincts."

Explanation: Self-confidence is bolstered by trusting both your abilities and instincts. This affirmation reinforces your belief in yourself and your decision-making skills.

Reflection Questions:

1. How did trusting your instincts help you today?
2. In what areas did you feel confident about your abilities?
3. How can you continue to build and maintain confidence in yourself?

Day 161: Affirmation for Positivity

Affirmation: "My positive attitude attracts wonderful experiences into my life."

Explanation: A positive attitude can bring about positive experiences. This affirmation encourages you to maintain an optimistic outlook, which in turn attracts favorable outcomes.

Reflection Questions:

1. What wonderful experiences did you attract today through your positive attitude?
2. How did maintaining positivity influence your interactions and events?
3. How can you continue to use positivity to draw in great

experiences?

Day 162: Affirmation for Security

Affirmation: "I am in control of creating a secure and stable environment for myself."

Explanation: Feeling in control of your environment contributes to security. This affirmation helps you take charge of creating a stable and secure space for yourself.

Reflection Questions:

1. What steps did you take to create a secure environment today?
2. How did your sense of control affect your feeling of stability?
3. How can you continue to enhance your ability to control and secure your environment?

Day 163: Affirmation for Wealth

Affirmation: "I attract financial opportunities that align with my values."

Explanation: Financial opportunities that align with your values are more fulfilling. This affirmation helps you attract and recognize opportunities that support both your financial goals and personal principles.

Reflection Questions:

1. What financial opportunities did you attract today that matched your values?
2. How did these opportunities align with your long-term goals?
3. How can you continue to seek and recognize opportunities that resonate with your values?

Day 164: Affirmation for Love

Affirmation: "I am a beacon of love and attract loving energy."

Explanation: Being a source of love attracts similar energy from others. This affirmation encourages you to radiate love, drawing in positive and loving interactions.

Reflection Questions:

1. How did you act as a beacon of love today?
2. What loving energy did you attract into your life?
3. How can you continue to radiate love and attract positive relationships?

Day 165: Affirmation for Purpose

Affirmation: "I am passionate about pursuing my purpose and fulfilling my potential."

Explanation: Passion fuels the pursuit of your purpose. This affirmation helps you stay motivated and enthusiastic about achieving your goals and realizing your potential.

Reflection Questions:

1. How did your passion drive you toward your purpose today?
2. What progress did you make in fulfilling your potential?
3. How can you maintain and strengthen your passion for your goals?

Day 166: Affirmation for Self-Confidence

Affirmation: "I embrace my uniqueness and the value it brings."

Explanation: Self-confidence is enhanced by embracing your unique qualities. This affirmation helps you recognize and appreciate the value of your individuality.

Reflection Questions:

1. How did you embrace your uniqueness today?
2. In what ways did your individuality contribute positively to your day?
3. How can you continue to celebrate and leverage your

unique qualities?

Day 167: Affirmation for Positivity

Affirmation: "I am a source of positivity and inspire others with my energy."

Explanation: Being a source of positivity not only benefits you but also inspires those around you. This affirmation encourages you to spread positive energy and uplift others.

Reflection Questions:

1. How did you act as a source of positivity today?
2. In what ways did your positive energy impact those around you?
3. How can you continue to inspire and uplift others with your positivity?

Day 168: Affirmation for Security

Affirmation: "I have the inner strength to create and maintain my sense of security."

Explanation: Inner strength is crucial for security. This affirmation helps you recognize and trust your own strength to build and sustain a secure environment.

Reflection Questions:

1. How did your inner strength help you maintain security today?
2. What aspects of your life felt more secure due to your efforts?
3. How can you further develop your inner strength to enhance your sense of security?

Day 169: Affirmation for Wealth

Affirmation: "I manage my finances wisely and make choices that support my wealth."

Explanation: Wise financial management is key to building and maintaining wealth. This affirmation encourages you to make thoughtful financial decisions that support long-term prosperity.

Reflection Questions:

1. What wise financial choices did you make today?
2. How did these choices support your wealth-building goals?
3. How can you continue to manage your finances effectively?

Day 170: Affirmation for Love

Affirmation: "I give and receive love freely and abundantly."

Explanation: Love is most fulfilling when given and received without limitations. This affirmation encourages you to engage in open and abundant expressions of love.

Reflection Questions:

1. How did you give and receive love freely today?
2. What impact did this open exchange of love have on your relationships?
3. How can you continue to foster a loving environment in your life?

Day 171: Affirmation for Purpose

Affirmation: "I am committed to my purpose and take deliberate steps to achieve it."

Explanation: Commitment and deliberate action are essential for fulfilling your purpose. This affirmation reinforces your dedication to making progress towards your goals.

Reflection Questions:

1. What deliberate steps did you take today towards your purpose?
2. How did your commitment affect your progress?
3. How can you maintain and strengthen your commitment to your purpose?

Day 172: Affirmation for Self-Confidence

Affirmation: "I trust my abilities and am confident in my decisions."

Explanation: Trusting your abilities and decisions enhances self-confidence. This affirmation helps you believe in your skills and choices, boosting your overall confidence.

Reflection Questions:

1. How did trusting your abilities and decisions influence your confidence today?
2. What decisions did you feel particularly confident about?
3. How can you build and maintain trust in your own abilities?

Day 173: Affirmation for Positivity

Affirmation: "I choose to focus on the positive aspects of every situation."

Explanation: Focusing on positive aspects helps maintain an optimistic outlook. This affirmation encourages you to seek and emphasize the good in any situation.

Reflection Questions:

1. What positive aspects did you focus on today?
2. How did this focus impact your mood and perspective?
3. How can you continue to shift your focus to the positive in challenging situations?

Day 174: Affirmation for Security

Affirmation: "I create a safe and stable environment for myself and those I care about."

Explanation: Creating a secure environment fosters a sense of safety. This affirmation helps you take responsibility for building and maintaining a stable space for yourself and loved ones.

Reflection Questions:

1. What steps did you take today to create a safe environment?
2. How did these efforts contribute to your sense of security and stability?
3. How can you enhance your ability to create a secure environment?

Day 175: Affirmation for Wealth

Affirmation: "I am open to receiving the wealth and abundance that life offers."

Explanation: Openness to receiving wealth is essential for attracting it. This affirmation helps you remain receptive to opportunities and prosperity that come your way.

Reflection Questions:

1. How did you open yourself to receiving wealth and abundance today?

2. What opportunities or experiences did you encounter as a result?
3. How can you stay open to receiving more in the future?

Day 176: Affirmation for Love

Affirmation: "I nurture loving relationships that bring joy and fulfillment."

Explanation: Nurturing loving relationships enhances joy and fulfillment. This affirmation encourages you to invest time and effort into relationships that add value to your life.

Reflection Questions:

1. How did you nurture your loving relationships today?
2. What joy and fulfillment did these relationships bring you?
3. How can you continue to cultivate and cherish these relationships?

Day 177: Affirmation for Purpose

Affirmation: "I am driven by my purpose and motivated to achieve my goals."

Explanation: A strong drive and motivation are key to pursuing your purpose. This affirmation reinforces your dedication and enthusiasm for achieving your goals.

Reflection Questions:

1. What motivated you to pursue your purpose today?
2. How did this drive influence your actions and progress?
3. How can you maintain and enhance your motivation for your goals?

Day 178: Affirmation for Self-Confidence

Affirmation: "I celebrate my strengths and embrace my growth."

Explanation: Celebrating your strengths and embracing growth fosters self-confidence. This affirmation encourages you to recognize and appreciate your personal development and achievements.

Reflection Questions:

1. What strengths did you celebrate today?
2. How did embracing your growth affect your self-confidence?
3. How can you regularly acknowledge and celebrate your progress?

Day 179: Affirmation for Positivity

Affirmation: "I approach each day with a hopeful and positive mindset."

Explanation: A hopeful and positive mindset sets the tone for a successful day. This affirmation helps you start each day with optimism and enthusiasm.

Reflection Questions:

1. How did your hopeful and positive mindset affect your day?
2. What challenges did you approach with this attitude, and what was the outcome?
3. How can you consistently cultivate and maintain a hopeful mindset?

Day 180: Affirmation for Security

Affirmation: "I am secure in my ability to create and maintain stability in my life."

Explanation: Confidence in your ability to create stability reinforces your sense of security. This affirmation supports your belief in your skills to manage and maintain a stable life.

Reflection Questions:

1. How did you demonstrate your ability to create stability today?
2. What aspects of your life felt more secure as a result?

3. How can you continue to enhance your ability to maintain stability?

Day 181: Affirmation for Wealth

Affirmation: "I am worthy of living a prosperous and abundant life."

Explanation: Believing in your worthiness is essential for attracting prosperity. This affirmation reinforces your self-worth and openness to living a life of abundance.

Reflection Questions:

1. How did you affirm your worthiness of prosperity today?
2. What actions or thoughts supported this belief?
3. How can you continue to embrace your worthiness of an abundant life?

Day 182: Affirmation for Love

Affirmation: "I am surrounded by love, and I attract positive, nurturing relationships."

Explanation: Being surrounded by love and attracting positive relationships enhances your emotional well-being. This affirmation encourages you to seek and foster nurturing connections.

Reflection Questions:

1. How did you experience and attract loving relationships today?
2. What positive impacts did these relationships have on you?
3. How can you continue to cultivate and attract nurturing connections?

Day 183: Affirmation for Purpose

Affirmation: "I am committed to living a life of purpose and making a difference."

Explanation: Commitment to living purposefully and making a difference fuels your sense of fulfillment. This affirmation reinforces your dedication to impactful living.

Reflection Questions:

1. What steps did you take today to live a purposeful life?
2. How did these actions contribute to making a difference?
3. How can you further align your daily actions with your sense of purpose?

Day 184: Affirmation for Self-Confidence

Affirmation: "I believe in my potential and trust in my journey."

Explanation: Believing in your potential and trusting your journey builds self-confidence. This affirmation supports your faith in your abilities and the path you're on.

Reflection Questions:

1. How did believing in your potential influence your actions today?
2. In what ways did trusting your journey affect your confidence?
3. How can you reinforce your belief in your potential and journey?

Day 185: Affirmation for Positivity

Affirmation: "I radiate positivity and attract positive energy into my life."

Explanation: Radiating positivity attracts similar energy from others and experiences. This affirmation helps you cultivate and spread positive energy in your environment.

Reflection Questions:

1. How did you radiate positivity today?
2. What positive energy or experiences did you attract?
3. How can you continue to spread and attract positive

energy?

Day 186: Affirmation for Security

Affirmation: "I trust in my ability to create a secure and stable future."

Explanation: Trusting your ability to build a secure future fosters a sense of stability. This affirmation supports your confidence in your capacity to shape and sustain a stable future.

Reflection Questions:

1. How did you demonstrate trust in your ability to create stability today?
2. What aspects of your future felt more secure as a result?
3. How can you continue to build and trust in your vision for a secure future?

Day 187: Affirmation for Wealth

Affirmation: "I attract opportunities that align with my financial goals and values."

Explanation: Attracting opportunities that align with your goals and values supports financial success. This affirmation helps you recognize and seize opportunities that match your aspirations.

Reflection Questions:

1. What opportunities aligned with your financial goals did you attract today?
2. How did these opportunities fit with your values?
3. How can you continue to attract and pursue opportunities that support your goals?

Day 188: Affirmation for Love

Affirmation: "I am open to giving and receiving love without limitations."

Explanation: Being open to giving and receiving love without limitations fosters deeper connections and more fulfilling relationships. This affirmation encourages you to embrace love fully and without reservation.

Reflection Questions:

1. How did you open yourself to giving and receiving love today?
2. What experiences or interactions did you have as a result of this openness?
3. How can you further enhance your ability to love and be loved without limitations?

Day 189: Affirmation for Purpose

Affirmation: "I embrace each moment as an opportunity to fulfill my purpose."

Explanation: Viewing each moment as an opportunity for fulfilling your purpose helps you stay engaged and motivated. This affirmation encourages you to make the most of every opportunity to advance towards your goals.

Reflection Questions:

1. How did you embrace today as an opportunity to fulfill your purpose?
2. What moments or actions contributed to advancing your purpose?
3. How can you continue to see and use each moment as a chance to move closer to your goals?

Day 190: Affirmation for Self-Confidence

Affirmation: "I confidently express my true self and share my unique gifts with the world."

Explanation: Expressing your true self and sharing your unique gifts boosts self-confidence and allows you to make a positive impact. This affirmation supports your authenticity and encourages you to showcase your strengths.

Reflection Questions:

1. In what ways did you express your true self today?

2. How did sharing your unique gifts impact your confidence and interactions?
3. How can you continue to confidently share and celebrate your unique qualities?

Day 191: Affirmation for Positivity

Affirmation: "I focus on what I can control and let go of what I cannot."

Explanation: Focusing on what you can control helps maintain a positive mindset and reduces stress. This affirmation encourages you to let go of what is beyond your control and concentrate on positive actions.

Reflection Questions:

1. What aspects of your life did you focus on today that you can control?
2. How did letting go of what you cannot control affect your positivity?
3. How can you continue to differentiate between what you can and cannot control?

Day 192: Affirmation for Security

Affirmation: "I am proactive in creating security and stability in all areas of my life."

Explanation: Being proactive in creating security and stability reinforces your sense of control and safety. This affirmation encourages you to take deliberate actions to enhance your security.

Reflection Questions:

1. What proactive steps did you take today to create security and stability?
2. How did these actions impact your sense of security in different areas of your life?
3. How can you maintain a proactive approach to building and sustaining stability?

Day 193: Affirmation for Wealth

Affirmation: "I am grateful for the wealth I have and excited for the abundance that is coming."

Explanation: Gratitude for existing wealth and excitement for future abundance enhances your overall attitude towards wealth. This affirmation fosters a positive outlook on your financial journey.

Reflection Questions:

1. What aspects of your current wealth are you grateful for

today?

2. How did your excitement for future abundance influence your mindset?

3. How can you maintain gratitude and excitement for both current and future wealth?

Day 194: Affirmation for Love

Affirmation: "I attract loving and supportive people who enhance my life."

Explanation: Attracting loving and supportive people enriches your life and strengthens your relationships. This affirmation encourages you to surround yourself with positive influences.

Reflection Questions:

1. How did you attract loving and supportive people today?
2. What positive effects did these people have on your life?
3. How can you continue to foster and attract supportive relationships?

Day 195: Affirmation for Purpose

Affirmation: "I am clear about my purpose and take inspired action towards it every day."

Explanation: Clarity about your purpose and taking inspired action are crucial for achieving your goals. This affirmation helps you stay focused and motivated in your pursuit of purpose.

Reflection Questions:

1. How did you gain clarity about your purpose today?
2. What inspired actions did you take towards fulfilling your purpose?
3. How can you continue to gain clarity and take effective action?

Day 196: Affirmation for Self-Confidence

Affirmation: "I recognize my achievements and use them as a foundation for further success."

Explanation: Recognizing your achievements boosts self-confidence and provides a strong foundation for future success. This affirmation encourages you to build on your past accomplishments.

Reflection Questions:

1. What achievements did you recognize and celebrate today?

2. How did these achievements contribute to your confidence and future plans?
3. How can you use past successes as a foundation for continued growth?

Day 197: Affirmation for Positivity

Affirmation: "I choose to see the best in every situation and find opportunities in challenges."

Explanation: Choosing to see the best in every situation helps maintain a positive outlook and find opportunities in challenges. This affirmation encourages a constructive approach to difficulties.

Reflection Questions:

1. How did you find the best aspects of situations today?
2. What opportunities did you identify in challenges you faced?
3. How can you continue to adopt this positive perspective in your daily life?

Day 198: Affirmation for Security

Affirmation: "I build a solid foundation of security through my actions and decisions."

Explanation: Building a solid foundation of security involves making deliberate and thoughtful decisions. This affirmation reinforces the importance of your actions in creating stability.

Reflection Questions:

1. What actions and decisions did you make today to build security?
2. How did these choices contribute to your overall sense of stability?
3. How can you ensure that your actions consistently support your security?

Day 199: Affirmation for Wealth

Affirmation: "I am capable of creating and growing my wealth with dedication and effort."

Explanation: Believing in your capability to create and grow wealth is essential for achieving financial success. This affirmation reinforces your dedication and effort in building wealth.

Reflection Questions:

1. What dedicated efforts did you make today towards creating wealth?

2. How did your belief in your capability influence your actions?
3. How can you continue to apply dedication and effort to grow your wealth?

Day 200: Affirmation for Love

Affirmation: "I offer my love and support to others, creating meaningful connections."

Explanation: Offering love and support to others strengthens connections and enhances relationships. This affirmation encourages you to contribute positively to your interactions with others.

Reflection Questions:

1. How did you offer love and support to others today?
2. What meaningful connections were created or strengthened as a result?
3. How can you continue to nurture these connections with love and support?

Day 201: Affirmation for Purpose

Affirmation: "I align my daily actions with my purpose and pursue it with passion."

Explanation: Aligning daily actions with your purpose and pursuing it with passion drives fulfillment and progress. This affirmation helps you stay committed and enthusiastic about your goals.

Reflection Questions:

1. How did you align your actions with your purpose today?
2. In what ways did passion influence your pursuit of your goals?
3. How can you maintain alignment and enthusiasm for your purpose?

Day 202: Affirmation for Self-Confidence

Affirmation: "I trust my intuition and follow it with confidence."

Explanation: Trusting your intuition and following it with confidence enhances self-assurance and decision-making. This affirmation supports your reliance on inner guidance.

Reflection Questions:

1. How did you trust and follow your intuition today?
2. What confidence did this trust bring to your decisions?
3. How can you continue to strengthen your reliance on your

intuition?

Day 203: Affirmation for Positivity

Affirmation: "I cultivate positivity by surrounding myself with uplifting influences."

Explanation: Surrounding yourself with uplifting influences helps maintain a positive mindset. This affirmation encourages you to seek and nurture positive environments and relationships.

Reflection Questions:

1. What uplifting influences did you surround yourself with today?
2. How did these influences impact your positivity and mood?
3. How can you continue to cultivate and embrace positive environments?

Day 204: Affirmation for Security

Affirmation: "I create security in my life by being proactive and prepared."

Explanation: Being proactive and prepared helps create a sense of security. This affirmation emphasizes the importance of planning and taking action to ensure stability.

Reflection Questions:

1. What proactive steps did you take today to create security?
2. How did preparation contribute to your sense of stability?
3. How can you enhance your proactive efforts to ensure continued security?

Day 205: Affirmation for Wealth

Affirmation: "I attract financial opportunities that align with my values and goals."

Explanation: Attracting financial opportunities that align with your values and goals supports meaningful wealth growth. This affirmation encourages you to seek opportunities that resonate with your financial aspirations.

Reflection Questions:

1. What financial opportunities aligned with your values and goals did you attract today?
2. How did these opportunities impact your financial journey?
3. How can you continue to attract and pursue opportunities that align with your goals?

Day 206: Affirmation for Love

Affirmation: "I am deserving of deep, unconditional love and embrace it fully."

Explanation: Believing in your worthiness of deep, unconditional love helps you embrace and receive love fully. This affirmation supports a strong sense of self-worth and openness to love.

Reflection Questions:

1. How did you acknowledge your worthiness of deep, unconditional love today?
2. In what ways did you embrace and experience this love in your life?
3. How can you continue to cultivate and accept this kind of love?

Day 207: Affirmation for Purpose

Affirmation: "I follow my purpose with unwavering commitment and determination."

Explanation: Unwavering commitment and determination towards your purpose ensure progress and fulfillment. This affirmation reinforces your dedication to pursuing your goals with persistence.

Reflection Questions:

1. How did you demonstrate commitment and determina-

tion towards your purpose today?

2. What progress did you make as a result of your dedication?
3. How can you maintain this level of commitment and determination in the future?

Day 208: Affirmation for Self-Confidence

Affirmation: "I celebrate my progress and use it as motivation to continue growing."

Explanation: Celebrating progress boosts self-confidence and motivates further growth. This affirmation encourages you to recognize and appreciate your achievements as a source of inspiration.

Reflection Questions:

1. What progress did you celebrate today?
2. How did this celebration impact your motivation and self-confidence?
3. How can you use your progress as a foundation for continued growth?

Day 209: Affirmation for Positivity

Affirmation: "I choose to focus on solutions rather than dwelling on problems."

Explanation: Focusing on solutions rather than problems promotes a positive and proactive mindset. This affirmation encourages you to shift your attention to finding constructive ways to address challenges.

Reflection Questions:

1. What solutions did you focus on today instead of problems?
2. How did this focus affect your overall positivity and mindset?
3. How can you continue to adopt a solution-oriented approach to challenges?

Day 210: Affirmation for Security

Affirmation: "I establish a sense of security through self-care and mindful practices."

Explanation: Self-care and mindful practices contribute to a sense of personal security and well-being. This affirmation highlights the importance of taking care of yourself to maintain stability and peace.

Reflection Questions:

1. What self-care and mindful practices did you incorporate

into your routine today?

2. How did these practices contribute to your sense of security and well-being?

3. How can you continue to prioritize self-care and mindfulness in your life?

Day 211: Affirmation for Wealth

Affirmation: "I am open to receiving wealth from unexpected sources with gratitude."

Explanation: Being open to receiving wealth from unexpected sources and expressing gratitude enhances your financial abundance. This affirmation helps you remain receptive to various opportunities.

Reflection Questions:

1. How did you remain open to receiving wealth from unexpected sources today?

2. What unexpected opportunities or resources came your way?

3. How can you continue to cultivate openness and gratitude for financial abundance?

Day 212: Affirmation for Love

Affirmation: "I nurture loving relationships by being present and attentive."

Explanation: Being present and attentive in your relationships fosters deeper connections and mutual respect. This affirmation encourages you to actively engage in and nurture your relationships.

Reflection Questions:

1. How did you practice being present and attentive in your relationships today?
2. What positive changes or deepening of connections resulted from this presence?
3. How can you consistently nurture your relationships through presence and attentiveness?

Day 213: Affirmation for Purpose

Affirmation: "I take inspired action towards my purpose with faith and enthusiasm."

Explanation: Taking inspired action with faith and enthusiasm propels you towards achieving your purpose. This affirmation encourages you to act with conviction and excitement in your endeavors.

Reflection Questions:

1. What inspired actions did you take towards your purpose

today?

2. How did faith and enthusiasm influence your efforts and progress?
3. How can you maintain this level of inspiration and excitement in your pursuits?

Day 214: Affirmation for Self-Confidence

Affirmation: "I trust in my abilities and confidently tackle new challenges."

Explanation: Trusting in your abilities and tackling new challenges with confidence strengthens self-assurance. This affirmation supports your readiness to face new opportunities with a positive attitude.

Reflection Questions:

1. What new challenges did you tackle with confidence today?
2. How did trusting in your abilities affect your approach to these challenges?
3. How can you continue to build and maintain confidence in your abilities?

Day 215: Affirmation for Positivity

Affirmation: "I embrace change with a positive outlook and adapt gracefully."

Explanation: Embracing change with a positive outlook helps you adapt gracefully and find opportunities in transitions. This affirmation encourages a flexible and optimistic attitude towards change.

Reflection Questions:

1. How did you embrace and adapt to changes today?
2. What positive outcomes resulted from your outlook on these changes?
3. How can you continue to cultivate a positive attitude towards future changes?

Day 216: Affirmation for Security

Affirmation: "I build my security by setting clear boundaries and maintaining balance."

Explanation: Setting clear boundaries and maintaining balance contributes to a strong sense of security. This affirmation highlights the importance of creating structure and equilibrium in your life.

Reflection Questions:

1. What boundaries did you set today to enhance your sense of security?

2. How did maintaining balance impact your overall stability and well-being?
3. How can you continue to establish and uphold boundaries to ensure security?

Day 217: Affirmation for Wealth

Affirmation: "I align my financial goals with my values and take purposeful steps towards them."

Explanation: Aligning financial goals with your values and taking purposeful steps ensures meaningful wealth growth. This affirmation encourages you to integrate your values into your financial planning and actions.

Reflection Questions:

1. How did you align your financial goals with your values today?
2. What purposeful steps did you take towards achieving these goals?
3. How can you ensure that your financial actions consistently reflect your values?

Day 218: Affirmation for Love

Affirmation: "I express my love openly and encourage others to do the same."

Explanation: Expressing love openly and encouraging others to reciprocate creates a nurturing and supportive environment. This affirmation promotes open communication and emotional sharing in relationships.

Reflection Questions:

1. How did you express your love openly today?
2. In what ways did you encourage others to share their love with you?
3. How can you continue to foster an environment of open emotional expression?

Day 219: Affirmation for Purpose

Affirmation: "I am committed to my purpose and take deliberate actions that reflect my dedication."

Explanation: Commitment to your purpose and taking deliberate actions reflect your dedication and drive. This affirmation supports a focused and intentional approach to achieving your goals.

Reflection Questions:

1. What deliberate actions did you take today that reflected your commitment to your purpose?

178

2. How did these actions influence your progress and motivation?

3. How can you ensure that your actions consistently align with your dedication?

Day 220: Affirmation for Self-Confidence

Affirmation: "I embrace my uniqueness and stand proudly in my individuality."

Explanation: Embracing your uniqueness and standing proudly in your individuality reinforces self-confidence. This affirmation supports the celebration of your distinct qualities and personal strengths.

Reflection Questions:

1. How did you embrace and celebrate your uniqueness today?

2. In what ways did standing proudly in your individuality affect your confidence?

3. How can you continue to honor and express your individuality with pride?

Day 221: Affirmation for Positivity

Affirmation: "I choose to focus on the good in every situation and find joy in the little things."

Explanation: Focusing on the good and finding joy in the little things enhances your overall positivity. This affirmation encourages you to maintain a grateful and joyful perspective.

Reflection Questions:

1. How did you focus on the positive aspects of situations today?
2. What small joys did you find and appreciate in your daily life?
3. How can you continue to cultivate this positive and joyful mindset?

Day 222: Affirmation for Security

Affirmation: "I create a sense of security by being proactive in planning and staying organized."

Explanation: Proactive planning and staying organized contribute to a strong sense of security. This affirmation underscores the importance of structure and preparation in maintaining stability.

Reflection Questions:

1. What proactive planning and organizational efforts did you make today?

2. How did these efforts contribute to your overall sense of security?
3. How can you enhance your planning and organizational skills to ensure continued stability?

Day 223: Affirmation for Wealth

Affirmation: "I embrace opportunities to learn and grow financially with an open mind."

Explanation: Embracing opportunities for financial learning and growth with an open mind supports wealth development. This affirmation encourages a willingness to explore and expand your financial knowledge.

Reflection Questions:

1. What financial learning opportunities did you embrace today?
2. How did having an open mind impact your financial growth and development?
3. How can you continue to seek and utilize opportunities for financial learning?

Day 224: Affirmation for Love

Affirmation: "I surround myself with love and kindness, and I radiate these qualities to others."

Explanation: Surrounding yourself with love and kindness and radiating these qualities enhances relationships and creates a positive environment. This affirmation supports the cultivation of a loving and compassionate atmosphere.

Reflection Questions:

1. How did you surround yourself with love and kindness today?
2. In what ways did you radiate these qualities to others?
3. How can you continue to foster and spread love and kindness in your interactions?

Day 225: Affirmation for Purpose

Affirmation: "I trust the journey of my purpose and embrace each step with patience."

Explanation: Trusting the journey and embracing each step with patience allows you to navigate your purpose with grace. This affirmation encourages a balanced and trusting approach to your path.

Reflection Questions:

1. How did you trust and embrace the journey of your purpose today?

2. What steps did you take with patience and how did they influence your progress?
3. How can you continue to trust and patiently navigate your purpose?

Day 226: Affirmation for Self-Confidence

Affirmation: "I acknowledge my strengths and use them to overcome any obstacles."

Explanation: Acknowledging your strengths and using them to overcome obstacles builds self-confidence and resilience. This affirmation supports a proactive and empowered approach to challenges.

Reflection Questions:

1. What strengths did you acknowledge and utilize today?
2. How did these strengths help you overcome any obstacles you faced?
3. How can you continue to leverage your strengths in future challenges?

Day 227: Affirmation for Positivity

Affirmation: "I cultivate a mindset of gratitude and focus on the positives in every situation."

Explanation: Cultivating a mindset of gratitude and focusing on the positives promotes overall positivity and resilience. This affirmation encourages a grateful perspective that enhances your well-being.

Reflection Questions:

1. How did you cultivate gratitude and focus on positives today?
2. What positive outcomes resulted from this mindset?
3. How can you maintain and strengthen your gratitude practice?

Day 228: Affirmation for Security

Affirmation: "I build my security by nurturing my relationships and creating a supportive network."

Explanation: Nurturing relationships and creating a supportive network contribute to a sense of security and stability. This affirmation highlights the importance of strong, reliable connections in your life.

Reflection Questions:

1. How did you nurture your relationships and support network today?

2. In what ways did this contribute to your sense of security?
3. How can you continue to build and strengthen your supportive network?

Day 229: Affirmation for Wealth

Affirmation: "I manage my finances with wisdom and integrity, attracting lasting prosperity."

Explanation: Managing finances with wisdom and integrity ensures lasting prosperity and financial health. This affirmation supports responsible and ethical financial practices.

Reflection Questions:

1. How did you manage your finances with wisdom and integrity today?
2. What impact did this approach have on your financial well-being?
3. How can you continue to practice financial wisdom and integrity?

Day 230: Affirmation for Love

Affirmation: "I create space for love by letting go of past hurts and embracing the present."

Explanation: Letting go of past hurts and embracing the

present allows you to create space for new and fulfilling love. This affirmation supports healing and openness in your relationships.

Reflection Questions:

1. How did you let go of past hurts and embrace the present today?
2. What positive changes did you notice in your capacity for love?
3. How can you continue to foster healing and openness in your relationships?

Day 231: Affirmation for Purpose

Affirmation: "I align my actions with my values and stay true to my purpose with clarity."

Explanation: Aligning actions with values and staying true to your purpose ensures that you live authentically and with clarity. This affirmation reinforces your commitment to meaningful and value-driven goals.

Reflection Questions:

1. How did you align your actions with your values today?
2. In what ways did this alignment support your clarity and purpose?
3. How can you continue to live authentically and stay true to your purpose?

Day 232: Affirmation for Self-Confidence

Affirmation: "I take pride in my achievements and use them as a foundation for future success."

Explanation: Taking pride in your achievements and using them as a foundation for future success reinforces self-confidence and motivation. This affirmation supports a positive self-view and goal-setting.

Reflection Questions:

1. What achievements did you take pride in today?
2. How did these achievements impact your sense of self-confidence?
3. How can you use your achievements to support future successes?

Day 233: Affirmation for Positivity

Affirmation: "I maintain a positive attitude by focusing on what I can control and letting go of what I cannot."

Explanation: Focusing on what you can control and letting go of what you cannot helps maintain a positive attitude. This affirmation encourages a balanced and constructive approach to challenges.

Reflection Questions:

1. What aspects of your life did you focus on controlling today?

2. How did letting go of what you cannot control affect your positivity?
3. How can you continue to manage your attitude by focusing on controllable aspects?

Day 234: Affirmation for Security

Affirmation: "I create a secure environment for myself by practicing self-care and setting healthy boundaries."

Explanation: Practicing self-care and setting healthy boundaries contribute to a secure and stable environment. This affirmation emphasizes the importance of taking care of yourself and maintaining clear limits.

Reflection Questions:

1. What self-care practices and boundaries did you implement today?
2. How did these practices contribute to your sense of security?
3. How can you continue to prioritize self-care and healthy boundaries?

Day 235: Affirmation for Wealth

Affirmation: "I attract wealth by maintaining a positive mindset and taking proactive steps towards my financial goals."

Explanation: Maintaining a positive mindset and taking proactive steps towards financial goals attracts wealth and prosperity. This affirmation supports a proactive and optimistic approach to financial success.

Reflection Questions:

1. How did you maintain a positive mindset towards your financial goals today?
2. What proactive steps did you take towards achieving these goals?
3. How can you continue to blend positivity with proactive financial actions?

Day 236: Affirmation for Love

Affirmation: "I honor my relationships by being honest, respectful, and loving in all interactions."

Explanation: Being honest, respectful, and loving in all interactions strengthens and honors your relationships. This affirmation encourages integrity and kindness in your connections with others.

Reflection Questions:

189

1. How did you demonstrate honesty, respect, and love in your relationships today?
2. What effects did this approach have on your interactions and connections?
3. How can you continue to uphold these values in your relationships?

Day 237: Affirmation for Purpose

Affirmation: "I remain focused on my purpose by setting clear intentions and taking consistent action."

Explanation: Setting clear intentions and taking consistent action helps you stay focused on your purpose. This affirmation reinforces your commitment to purposeful and goal-oriented actions.

Reflection Questions:

1. What clear intentions did you set today for your purpose?
2. How did consistent action support your focus and progress?
3. How can you refine your intentions and actions to enhance your focus on purpose?

Day 238: Affirmation for Self-Confidence

Affirmation: "I celebrate my growth and embrace the journey of becoming my best self."

Explanation: Celebrating growth and embracing the journey of self-improvement enhances self-confidence and self-acceptance. This affirmation supports a positive view of your ongoing development.

Reflection Questions:

1. What aspects of your growth did you celebrate today?
2. How did embracing your journey impact your self-confidence and self-acceptance?
3. How can you continue to celebrate and embrace your personal development?

Day 239: Affirmation for Positivity

Affirmation: "I radiate positivity and inspire others to see the good in every situation."

Explanation: Radiating positivity and inspiring others to see the good fosters a positive environment and uplifts those around you. This affirmation encourages you to be a source of positivity and inspiration.

Reflection Questions:

1. How did you radiate positivity and inspire others today?
2. What reactions or changes did you observe in others as a

result of your positivity?

3. How can you continue to be a positive influence and source of inspiration?

Day 240: Affirmation for Security

Affirmation: "I build a secure foundation by making informed decisions and planning for the future."

Explanation: Making informed decisions and planning for the future contribute to a secure foundation. This affirmation supports thoughtful decision-making and proactive planning for stability.

Reflection Questions:

1. What informed decisions did you make today?
2. How did planning for the future contribute to your sense of security?
3. How can you enhance your decision-making and planning to strengthen your security?

Day 241: Affirmation for Wealth

Affirmation: "I am grateful for the abundance in my life and open to receiving even more."

Explanation: Gratitude for current abundance and openness to receiving more attracts further wealth and prosperity. This affirmation supports a mindset of appreciation and receptivity.

Reflection Questions:

1. What aspects of abundance were you grateful for today?
2. How did your openness to receiving more affect your financial outlook?
3. How can you maintain and enhance your gratitude and receptivity for abundance?

Day 242: Affirmation for Love

Affirmation: "I nurture my heart by cultivating compassion and understanding in all my relationships."

Explanation: Cultivating compassion and understanding nurtures your heart and deepens your relationships. This affirmation promotes emotional growth and connection.

Reflection Questions:

1. How did you cultivate compassion and understanding in your relationships today?
2. What impact did this approach have on your interactions with others?
3. How can you further nurture your heart through compassion and understanding?

Day 243: Affirmation for Purpose

Affirmation: "I embrace new opportunities that align with my purpose and help me grow."

Explanation: Embracing new opportunities that align with your purpose supports personal growth and alignment with your goals. This affirmation encourages an open and receptive attitude towards new possibilities.

Reflection Questions:

1. What new opportunities did you embrace today that aligned with your purpose?
2. How did these opportunities contribute to your growth and alignment with your goals?
3. How can you continue to seek and embrace opportunities that support your purpose?

Day 244: Affirmation for Self-Confidence

Affirmation: "I trust in my abilities and face challenges with courage and determination."

Explanation: Trusting in your abilities and approaching challenges with courage and determination boosts self-confidence and resilience. This affirmation encourages a proactive and positive approach to overcoming obstacles.

Reflection Questions:

1. How did you trust in your abilities and approach chal-

lenges today?
2. What effects did your courage and determination have on your self-confidence?
3. How can you continue to build trust in your abilities and tackle challenges with confidence?

Day 245: Affirmation for Positivity

Affirmation: "I focus on solutions rather than problems, fostering a positive and proactive mindset."

Explanation: Focusing on solutions rather than problems promotes a positive and proactive mindset. This affirmation encourages constructive thinking and problem-solving.

Reflection Questions:

1. How did you focus on solutions rather than problems today?
2. What positive changes resulted from this approach?
3. How can you further cultivate a solution-oriented mindset in your daily life?

Day 246: Affirmation for Security

Affirmation: "I create a sense of security by staying grounded and resilient in the face of uncertainty."

Explanation: Staying grounded and resilient in the face of uncertainty enhances your sense of security. This affirmation supports stability and adaptability during challenging times.

Reflection Questions:

1. How did you stay grounded and resilient in the face of uncertainty today?
2. What effects did this approach have on your sense of security?
3. How can you continue to build and maintain resilience during uncertain times?

Day 247: Affirmation for Wealth

Affirmation: "I attract financial abundance by aligning my actions with my long-term goals and values."

Explanation: Aligning your actions with long-term goals and values attracts financial abundance and success. This affirmation supports a strategic and value-driven approach to wealth-building.

Reflection Questions:

1. How did you align your actions with your long-term goals and values today?

2. What impact did this alignment have on your financial outlook?
3. How can you refine your actions and goals to enhance financial abundance?

Day 248: Affirmation for Love

Affirmation: "I express my love openly and authentically, building deeper connections with those around me."

Explanation: Expressing love openly and authentically strengthens connections and fosters deeper relationships. This affirmation promotes honest and heartfelt communication in your interactions.

Reflection Questions:

1. How did you express your love openly and authentically today?
2. What effects did this expression have on your relationships and connections?
3. How can you continue to communicate your love in an open and genuine way?

Day 249: Affirmation for Purpose

Affirmation: "I stay committed to my purpose by celebrating my progress and setting new goals."

Explanation: Celebrating progress and setting new goals keeps you committed to your purpose and encourages ongoing growth. This affirmation supports a balanced approach to goal-setting and achievement.

Reflection Questions:

1. What progress did you celebrate today towards your purpose?
2. What new goals did you set, and how do they align with your purpose?
3. How can you continue to celebrate progress and set effective goals?

Day 250: Affirmation for Self-Confidence

Affirmation: "I value my unique contributions and confidently share my talents with the world."

Explanation: Valuing your unique contributions and sharing your talents with confidence enhances self-esteem and self-worth. This affirmation encourages a positive self-view and assertive expression of your abilities.

Reflection Questions:

1. What unique contributions did you value and share today?

2. How did sharing your talents impact your self-confidence and interactions?
3. How can you continue to recognize and express your unique abilities?

Day 251: Affirmation for Positivity

Affirmation: "I choose to see the good in every experience, fostering a mindset of optimism and joy."

Explanation: Choosing to see the good in every experience promotes a mindset of optimism and joy. This affirmation supports a positive perspective and emotional well-being.

Reflection Questions:

1. How did you choose to see the good in your experiences today?
2. What effects did this positive perspective have on your mood and outlook?
3. How can you maintain and strengthen your optimistic mindset?

Day 252: Affirmation for Security

Affirmation: "I cultivate a secure life by investing in my well-being and nurturing my personal growth."

Explanation: Investing in your well-being and nurturing personal growth enhances your overall sense of security. This affirmation supports a proactive approach to self-care and development.

Reflection Questions:

1. How did you invest in your well-being and personal growth today?
2. What impact did these investments have on your sense of security?
3. How can you continue to prioritize and support your well-being and growth?

Day 253: Affirmation for Wealth

Affirmation: "I manage my resources wisely, creating opportunities for sustainable and long-term prosperity."

Explanation: Managing resources wisely creates opportunities for sustainable and long-term prosperity. This affirmation supports a thoughtful and strategic approach to financial management.

Reflection Questions:

1. How did you manage your resources wisely today?

2. What opportunities for prosperity did this approach create?
3. How can you refine your resource management strategies for sustainable success?

Day 254: Affirmation for Love

Affirmation: "I foster love by being present, attentive, and supportive in my relationships."

Explanation: Being present, attentive, and supportive enhances the quality of your relationships and fosters love. This affirmation encourages active engagement and care in your interactions.

Reflection Questions:

1. How did you demonstrate presence, attentiveness, and support in your relationships today?
2. What effects did these actions have on your relationships and connections?
3. How can you continue to foster love through active and supportive engagement?

Day 255: Affirmation for Purpose

Affirmation: "I align my daily actions with my deeper purpose, creating a life of fulfillment and meaning."

Explanation: Aligning daily actions with your deeper purpose creates a sense of fulfillment and meaning in life. This affirmation supports a purposeful and intentional approach to daily activities.

Reflection Questions:

1. How did you align your daily actions with your deeper purpose today?
2. What sense of fulfillment and meaning did this alignment bring to your life?
3. How can you continue to integrate your purpose into your daily routine?

Day 256: Affirmation for Self-Confidence

Affirmation: "I recognize and embrace my growth, knowing that I am continuously evolving and improving."

Explanation: Recognizing and embracing your growth supports self-confidence and personal development. This affirmation promotes a positive view of your ongoing evolution and progress.

Reflection Questions:

1. What aspects of your growth did you recognize and

embrace today?

2. How did acknowledging your evolution impact your self-confidence?

3. How can you continue to support and celebrate your personal development?

Day 257: Affirmation for Positivity

Affirmation: "I attract positive energy by maintaining an open heart and a joyful attitude."

Explanation: Maintaining an open heart and joyful attitude attracts positive energy and enhances your overall outlook. This affirmation supports a vibrant and optimistic approach to life.

Reflection Questions:

1. How did you maintain an open heart and joyful attitude today?

2. What positive energy did you attract as a result?

3. How can you continue to foster and attract positive energy in your life?

Day 258: Affirmation for Security

Affirmation: "I strengthen my sense of security by creating stability through thoughtful planning and self-care."

Explanation: Creating stability through thoughtful planning and self-care enhances your sense of security. This affirmation supports a proactive approach to building a secure and balanced life.

Reflection Questions:

1. How did you create stability through planning and self-care today?
2. What impact did these actions have on your sense of security?
3. How can you continue to build and maintain stability in your life?

Day 259: Affirmation for Wealth

Affirmation: "I attract and manage wealth by staying focused on my goals and maintaining a positive financial mindset."

Explanation: Staying focused on your goals and maintaining a positive financial mindset helps attract and manage wealth. This affirmation supports a goal-oriented and optimistic approach to financial success.

Reflection Questions:

1. How did you stay focused on your financial goals today?

2. What impact did maintaining a positive mindset have on your financial situation?
3. How can you continue to blend focus and positivity in your approach to wealth?

Day 260: Affirmation for Love

Affirmation: "I create loving connections by actively listening, showing appreciation, and expressing gratitude."

Explanation: Actively listening, showing appreciation, and expressing gratitude strengthen loving connections. This affirmation encourages attentive communication and appreciation in relationships.

Reflection Questions:

1. How did you actively listen and show appreciation in your relationships today?
2. What impact did expressing gratitude have on your connections with others?
3. How can you continue to build loving connections through these practices?

Day 261: Affirmation for Purpose

Affirmation: "I take inspired action towards my purpose, trusting that each step brings me closer to my goals."

Explanation: Taking inspired action and trusting in each step supports progress towards your purpose. This affirmation encourages confidence in your journey and belief in your goals.

Reflection Questions:

1. What inspired actions did you take towards your purpose today?
2. How did trusting in each step impact your progress towards your goals?
3. How can you maintain trust and inspiration in your pursuit of purpose?

Day 262: Affirmation for Self-Confidence

Affirmation: "I embrace my strengths and use them to overcome challenges and achieve my goals."

Explanation: Embracing your strengths and using them to overcome challenges enhances self-confidence and goal achievement. This affirmation promotes a positive self-view and proactive problem-solving.

Reflection Questions:

1. What strengths did you embrace and use to overcome challenges today?

2. How did this approach affect your confidence and progress towards your goals?
3. How can you continue to utilize your strengths effectively in future challenges?

Day 263: Affirmation for Positivity

Affirmation: "I cultivate a positive environment by surrounding myself with uplifting influences and thoughts."

Explanation: Surrounding yourself with uplifting influences and thoughts fosters a positive environment. This affirmation supports a proactive approach to maintaining a positive mindset.

Reflection Questions:

1. What uplifting influences and thoughts did you surround yourself with today?
2. How did these influences affect your overall positivity and environment?
3. How can you continue to create and maintain a positive environment?

Day 264: Affirmation for Security

Affirmation: "I enhance my sense of security by setting clear boundaries and maintaining healthy relationships."

Explanation: Setting clear boundaries and maintaining healthy relationships supports a strong sense of security. This affirmation encourages self-respect and stability in your interactions.

Reflection Questions:

1. How did you set boundaries and maintain healthy relationships today?
2. What effects did these actions have on your sense of security?
3. How can you continue to establish and uphold boundaries to ensure security?

Day 265: Affirmation for Wealth

Affirmation: "I cultivate financial abundance by making mindful choices and aligning my spending with my values."

Explanation: Making mindful choices and aligning spending with your values supports financial abundance. This affirmation encourages conscious financial decisions and alignment with personal values.

Reflection Questions:

1. What mindful choices did you make in your financial

decisions today?

2. How did aligning your spending with your values impact your financial outlook?
3. How can you refine your financial choices to better align with your values?

Day 266: Affirmation for Love

Affirmation: "I deepen my relationships by being authentic, sharing openly, and embracing vulnerability."

Explanation: Being authentic, sharing openly, and embracing vulnerability strengthen and deepen relationships. This affirmation promotes genuine connections and emotional intimacy.

Reflection Questions:

1. How did you practice authenticity, openness, and vulnerability in your relationships today?
2. What impact did these practices have on your connections with others?
3. How can you continue to deepen relationships through these approaches?

Day 267: Affirmation for Purpose

Affirmation: "I remain focused on my purpose by regularly reviewing and adjusting my goals as needed."

Explanation: Regularly reviewing and adjusting your goals helps you stay focused on your purpose. This affirmation supports ongoing alignment and adaptability in your journey.

Reflection Questions:

1. How did you review and adjust your goals to stay aligned with your purpose today?
2. What effects did this process have on your focus and progress?
3. How can you incorporate regular goal reviews into your routine?

Day 268: Affirmation for Self-Confidence

Affirmation: "I confidently embrace new opportunities, knowing that each experience contributes to my growth."

Explanation: Embracing new opportunities with confidence supports personal growth and development. This affirmation encourages a positive and open approach to new experiences.

Reflection Questions:

1. What new opportunities did you embrace with confidence today?
2. How did these opportunities contribute to your personal

growth?

3. How can you continue to approach new experiences with confidence?

Day 269: Affirmation for Positivity

Affirmation: "I choose to focus on the positive aspects of my life, cultivating joy and gratitude daily."

Explanation: Focusing on the positive aspects of life fosters joy and gratitude. This affirmation supports a daily practice of positivity and appreciation.

Reflection Questions:

1. What positive aspects of your life did you focus on today?
2. How did this focus on positivity affect your overall mood and outlook?
3. How can you further enhance your daily practice of joy and gratitude?

Day 270: Affirmation for Security

Affirmation: "I build a strong foundation of security by staying grounded in my values and taking proactive steps."

Explanation: Staying grounded in your values and taking proactive steps supports a strong sense of security. This affirmation encourages stability and intentionality in your actions.

Reflection Questions:

1. How did you stay grounded in your values and take proactive steps today?
2. What impact did these actions have on your sense of security?
3. How can you continue to build and maintain a strong foundation of security?

Day 271: Affirmation for Wealth

Affirmation: "I attract wealth by embracing opportunities for growth and being open to receiving abundance."

Explanation: Embracing opportunities for growth and being open to receiving abundance helps attract wealth. This affirmation encourages a receptive and proactive approach to financial prosperity.

Reflection Questions:

1. What opportunities for growth did you embrace today?
2. How did being open to receiving abundance impact your financial outlook?
3. How can you continue to attract wealth through openness and growth?

Day 272: Affirmation for Love

Affirmation: "I create a loving environment by practicing kindness, empathy, and respect in all my interactions."

Explanation: Practicing kindness, empathy, and respect creates a loving environment. This affirmation supports positive and nurturing interactions with others.

Reflection Questions:

1. How did you practice kindness, empathy, and respect in your interactions today?
2. What effects did these practices have on your relationships and environment?
3. How can you continue to foster a loving environment through these behaviors?

Day 273: Affirmation for Purpose

Affirmation: "I stay connected to my purpose by seeking inspiration and aligning my actions with my vision."

Explanation: Seeking inspiration and aligning actions with your vision helps you stay connected to your purpose. This affirmation encourages a proactive approach to maintaining alignment with your goals.

Reflection Questions:

1. How did you seek inspiration and align your actions with your vision today?

2. What impact did this alignment have on your connection to your purpose?
3. How can you continue to stay connected to your purpose through inspiration and alignment?

Day 274: Affirmation for Self-Confidence

Affirmation: "I am confident in my unique path and embrace each challenge as an opportunity for growth."

Explanation: Being confident in your unique path and embracing challenges as opportunities for growth supports self-confidence and personal development. This affirmation promotes a positive and resilient mindset.

Reflection Questions:

1. How did you embrace challenges as opportunities for growth today?
2. What impact did this approach have on your confidence and development?
3. How can you continue to view challenges as opportunities in your journey?

Day 275: Affirmation for Positivity

Affirmation: "I radiate positivity by nurturing my inner joy and sharing it with those around me."

Explanation: Nurturing inner joy and sharing it with others helps radiate positivity. This affirmation supports an outward expression of happiness and a positive influence on those around you.

Reflection Questions:

1. How did you nurture your inner joy and share it with others today?
2. What effects did radiating positivity have on your interactions and environment?
3. How can you continue to cultivate and share joy to enhance positivity?

Day 276: Affirmation for Security

Affirmation: "I reinforce my sense of security by taking responsibility for my well-being and making informed decisions."

Explanation: Taking responsibility for your well-being and making informed decisions strengthens your sense of security. This affirmation supports a proactive and thoughtful approach to personal stability.

Reflection Questions:

1. How did you take responsibility for your well-being and make informed decisions today?
2. What impact did these actions have on your sense of security?
3. How can you continue to enhance your security through responsible and informed choices?

Day 277: Affirmation for Wealth

Affirmation: "I grow my financial wealth by setting clear intentions and taking consistent, deliberate actions."

Explanation: Setting clear intentions and taking consistent, deliberate actions supports financial growth and wealth. This affirmation encourages a focused and strategic approach to achieving financial goals.

Reflection Questions:

1. What clear intentions did you set for your financial goals today?
2. How did your deliberate actions contribute to your financial growth?
3. How can you maintain clarity and consistency in your approach to wealth-building?

Day 278: Affirmation for Love

Affirmation: "I build strong relationships by being present, listening actively, and showing genuine interest."

Explanation: Being present, listening actively, and showing genuine interest are key to building strong and meaningful relationships. This affirmation supports deeper connections and effective communication.

Reflection Questions:

1. How did you practice being present and listening actively in your interactions today?
2. What impact did showing genuine interest have on your relationships?
3. How can you continue to enhance your relationships through these practices?

Day 279: Affirmation for Purpose

Affirmation: "I stay motivated towards my purpose by celebrating small victories and learning from setbacks."

Explanation: Celebrating small victories and learning from setbacks helps maintain motivation towards your purpose. This affirmation promotes resilience and a positive outlook on progress.

Reflection Questions:

1. What small victories did you celebrate today, and how did

they motivate you?

2. How did you learn from any setbacks you encountered?
3. How can you use these strategies to stay motivated and focused on your purpose?

Day 280: Affirmation for Self-Confidence

Affirmation: "I trust in my abilities and am proud of my accomplishments, no matter how small."

Explanation: Trusting in your abilities and taking pride in your accomplishments, regardless of their size, boosts self-confidence. This affirmation supports self-acceptance and recognition of progress.

Reflection Questions:

1. What accomplishments did you recognize and feel proud of today?
2. How did trusting in your abilities affect your confidence?
3. How can you continue to acknowledge and celebrate your achievements?

Day 281: Affirmation for Positivity

Affirmation: "I foster positivity by focusing on solutions rather than dwelling on problems."

Explanation: Focusing on solutions instead of problems cultivates a positive mindset and proactive attitude. This affirmation supports constructive thinking and effective problem-solving.

Reflection Questions:

1. How did you focus on solutions rather than problems today?
2. What impact did this approach have on your overall positivity?
3. How can you maintain a solution-oriented mindset in future challenges?

Day 282: Affirmation for Security

Affirmation: "I build personal security by setting achievable goals and celebrating my progress along the way."

Explanation: Setting achievable goals and celebrating progress contribute to a sense of personal security. This affirmation encourages goal-setting and recognition of milestones.

Reflection Questions:

1. What achievable goals did you set and make progress on

today?

2. How did celebrating these milestones enhance your sense of security?

3. How can you continue to set and achieve goals to reinforce your personal security?

Day 283: Affirmation for Wealth

Affirmation: "I attract abundance by maintaining a positive mindset and being open to new opportunities."

Explanation: A positive mindset and openness to new opportunities help attract financial abundance. This affirmation encourages an optimistic approach to wealth-building.

Reflection Questions:

1. How did maintaining a positive mindset help you attract abundance today?

2. What new opportunities did you open yourself to?

3. How can you continue to foster an attitude of abundance and opportunity?

Day 284: Affirmation for Love

Affirmation: "I nurture my relationships by expressing appreciation and acknowledging the value of others."

Explanation: Expressing appreciation and acknowledging others' value strengthens relationships. This affirmation supports positive reinforcement and mutual respect in connections.

Reflection Questions:

1. How did you express appreciation and acknowledge others' value today?
2. What effects did these actions have on your relationships?
3. How can you continue to nurture your relationships through appreciation?

Day 285: Affirmation for Purpose

Affirmation: "I align my daily actions with my purpose, creating a sense of fulfillment and direction."

Explanation: Aligning daily actions with your purpose fosters a sense of fulfillment and direction. This affirmation supports intentional living and a clear focus on your goals.

Reflection Questions:

1. How did you align your daily actions with your purpose today?
2. What sense of fulfillment and direction did this alignment

provide?

3. How can you maintain alignment between your actions and purpose?

Day 286: Affirmation for Self-Confidence

Affirmation: "I embrace my journey with confidence, knowing that each step is a valuable part of my growth."

Explanation: Embracing your journey with confidence recognizes the value of each step in your growth process. This affirmation promotes a positive perspective on personal development.

Reflection Questions:

1. How did you embrace your journey with confidence today?
2. What value did you find in each step of your growth process?
3. How can you continue to approach your journey with confidence and positivity?

Day 287: Affirmation for Positivity

Affirmation: "I choose to see the good in every situation and use it as a source of strength."

Explanation: Seeing the good in every situation and using it as a source of strength enhances positivity and resilience. This affirmation supports a constructive and optimistic outlook.

Reflection Questions:

1. What good did you find in each situation you faced today?
2. How did focusing on the positive aspects provide strength and resilience?
3. How can you continue to view situations optimistically and use them to build strength?

Day 288: Affirmation for Security

Affirmation: "I reinforce my sense of security by creating and maintaining routines that support my well-being."

Explanation: Creating and maintaining routines that support your well-being reinforces your sense of security. This affirmation encourages structure and stability in your daily life.

Reflection Questions:

1. What routines did you create or maintain today to support your well-being?
2. How did these routines contribute to your sense of secu-

rity?

3. How can you continue to develop and uphold routines that reinforce your security?

Day 289: Affirmation for Wealth

Affirmation: "I grow my wealth by investing in myself and my future with intention and care."

Explanation: Investing in yourself and your future with intention and care supports financial growth. This affirmation encourages thoughtful and strategic actions towards wealth-building.

Reflection Questions:

1. How did you invest in yourself and your future today?
2. What impact did these investments have on your financial growth?
3. How can you continue to make intentional and caring investments in your future?

Day 290: Affirmation for Love

Affirmation: "I cultivate deep connections by being genuine, supportive, and understanding."

Explanation: Being genuine, supportive, and understanding fosters deep connections with others. This affirmation encourages authentic and empathetic interactions.

Reflection Questions:

1. How did you practice being genuine, supportive, and understanding today?
2. What effects did these qualities have on your relationships?
3. How can you continue to deepen connections through these behaviors?

Day 291: Affirmation for Purpose

Affirmation: "I stay committed to my purpose by embracing change and adapting to new challenges."

Explanation: Embracing change and adapting to new challenges helps maintain commitment to your purpose. This affirmation supports flexibility and resilience in pursuing your goals.

Reflection Questions:

1. How did you embrace change and adapt to challenges today?
2. What impact did this approach have on your commitment to your purpose?
3. How can you continue to stay committed to your purpose through adaptability?

Day 292: Affirmation for Self-Confidence

Affirmation: "I recognize and celebrate my progress, understanding that every step forward is a success."

Explanation: Recognizing and celebrating your progress supports self-confidence and acknowledges your achievements. This affirmation promotes a positive view of your journey.

Reflection Questions:

1. How did you recognize and celebrate your progress today?
2. How did acknowledging each step forward impact your confidence?
3. How can you continue to celebrate your achievements and maintain confidence?

Day 293: Affirmation for Positivity

Affirmation: "I actively seek out and embrace positive experiences, fostering a joyful and optimistic mindset."

Explanation: Seeking out and embracing positive experiences fosters joy and optimism. This affirmation encourages an active pursuit of positivity in your life.

Reflection Questions:

1. What positive experiences did you seek out and embrace today?
2. How did these experiences contribute to your overall

mindset?

3. How can you continue to actively cultivate positivity and joy in your life?

Day 294: Affirmation for Security

Affirmation: "I strengthen my sense of security by building supportive relationships and cultivating self-reliance."

Explanation: Building supportive relationships and cultivating self-reliance reinforce your sense of security. This affirmation encourages a balanced approach to personal and relational stability.

Reflection Questions:

1. How did you build supportive relationships and cultivate self-reliance today?
2. What effects did these actions have on your sense of security?
3. How can you continue to strengthen your security through these practices?

Day 295: Affirmation for Wealth

Affirmation: "I attract financial abundance by aligning my efforts with my values and staying persistent in my pursuits."

Explanation: Aligning efforts with your values and staying persistent helps attract financial abundance. This affirmation promotes a values-driven approach to wealth-building and perseverance.

Reflection Questions:

1. How did you align your efforts with your values today?
2. What role did persistence play in attracting financial abundance?
3. How can you continue to integrate values and persistence into your financial pursuits?

Day 296: Affirmation for Love

Affirmation: "I enhance my relationships by being present, offering support, and showing appreciation daily."

Explanation: Being present, offering support, and showing appreciation daily enhances relationships. This affirmation supports consistent and meaningful interactions with others.

Reflection Questions:

1. How did you practice being present, offering support, and showing appreciation today?
2. What impact did these actions have on your relationships?

3. How can you maintain these practices to continually enhance your connections?

Day 297: Affirmation for Purpose

Affirmation: "I fuel my purpose by setting clear intentions and taking inspired action towards my goals."

Explanation: Setting clear intentions and taking inspired action are key to fueling your purpose. This affirmation encourages a proactive and focused approach to achieving your goals.

Reflection Questions:

1. What clear intentions did you set for yourself today?
2. How did taking inspired action move you closer to your goals?
3. How can you refine your intentions and actions to better align with your purpose?

Day 298: Affirmation for Self-Confidence

Affirmation: "I embrace my unique strengths and talents, knowing they contribute to my success."

Explanation: Embracing your unique strengths and talents fosters self-confidence and acknowledges their role in your success. This affirmation supports self-acceptance and recognition of your abilities.

Reflection Questions:

1. What unique strengths and talents did you acknowledge today?
2. How did recognizing these attributes impact your confidence?
3. How can you continue to leverage your strengths and talents in your endeavors?

Day 299: Affirmation for Positivity

Affirmation: "I choose to focus on the positive aspects of every situation, finding opportunities for growth and learning."

Explanation: Focusing on positive aspects and finding opportunities for growth enhances a positive mindset. This affirmation promotes a constructive outlook on various situations.

Reflection Questions:

1. How did you focus on the positive aspects of situations today?
2. What opportunities for growth and learning did you identify?
3. How can you consistently apply this mindset to future challenges?

Day 300: Affirmation for Security

Affirmation: "I cultivate security by creating a stable foundation through planning, organization, and self-care."

Explanation: Creating a stable foundation through planning, organization, and self-care reinforces your sense of security. This affirmation encourages practical steps towards personal stability.

Reflection Questions:

1. How did you incorporate planning, organization, and self-care into your routine today?
2. How did these practices contribute to your sense of security?
3. What additional steps can you take to further cultivate stability and security?

Day 301: Affirmation for Wealth

Affirmation: "I manage my resources wisely and make informed decisions that enhance my financial well-being."

Explanation: Managing resources wisely and making informed decisions support financial well-being. This affirmation encourages thoughtful and strategic financial practices.

Reflection Questions:

1. How did you manage your resources and make informed decisions today?

2. What effects did these actions have on your financial well-being?

3. How can you improve your financial decision-making and resource management?

Day 302: Affirmation for Love

Affirmation: "I enrich my relationships by being authentic, expressing my feelings, and fostering open communication."

Explanation: Being authentic, expressing your feelings, and fostering open communication enrich relationships. This affirmation supports genuine and effective interaction with others.

Reflection Questions:

1. How did you practice authenticity, express your feelings, and foster communication today?

2. What impact did these practices have on your relationships?

3. How can you continue to nurture your relationships through these approaches?

Day 303: Affirmation for Purpose

Affirmation: "I advance my purpose by staying curious, embracing new experiences, and seeking continuous growth."

Explanation: Staying curious, embracing new experiences, and seeking continuous growth help advance your purpose. This affirmation supports an active and evolving pursuit of your goals.

Reflection Questions:

1. How did curiosity and new experiences contribute to your progress today?
2. What steps did you take towards continuous growth?
3. How can you maintain an attitude of curiosity and growth in pursuing your purpose?

Day 304: Affirmation for Self-Confidence

Affirmation: "I build my confidence by acknowledging my achievements and learning from every experience."

Explanation: Acknowledging achievements and learning from experiences build self-confidence. This affirmation promotes a positive view of your progress and growth.

Reflection Questions:

1. What achievements did you acknowledge today, and how did this impact your confidence?
2. How did you learn from your experiences and apply these

lessons?

3. How can you continue to build confidence through recognition and learning?

Day 305: Affirmation for Positivity

Affirmation: "I choose to surround myself with positive influences and engage in activities that uplift my spirit."

Explanation: Surrounding yourself with positive influences and engaging in uplifting activities enhance your positivity. This affirmation supports a joyful and inspiring environment.

Reflection Questions:

1. What positive influences and uplifting activities did you engage with today?
2. How did these experiences affect your overall positivity?
3. How can you continue to cultivate a positive environment in your life?

Day 306: Affirmation for Security

Affirmation: "I reinforce my security by taking proactive steps to manage risks and prepare for uncertainties."

Explanation: Managing risks and preparing for uncertainties enhance your sense of security. This affirmation

encourages proactive and thoughtful approaches to personal safety and stability.

Reflection Questions:

1. What proactive steps did you take to manage risks and prepare for uncertainties today?
2. How did these actions contribute to your sense of security?
3. What additional measures can you take to further enhance your personal security?

Day 307: Affirmation for Wealth

Affirmation: "I attract financial prosperity by aligning my actions with my values and being open to innovative opportunities."

Explanation: Aligning actions with values and being open to innovative opportunities attract financial prosperity. This affirmation supports ethical and creative approaches to wealth-building.

Reflection Questions:

1. How did aligning your actions with your values influence your financial situation today?
2. What innovative opportunities did you explore, and how did they impact your prosperity?
3. How can you continue to integrate values and creativity into your financial endeavors?

Day 308: Affirmation for Love

Affirmation: "I deepen my relationships by being attentive, empathetic, and offering consistent support."

Explanation: Being attentive, empathetic, and offering consistent support deepens relationships. This affirmation encourages meaningful and supportive interactions with others.

Reflection Questions:

1. How did you demonstrate attentiveness, empathy, and support in your relationships today?
2. What effects did these behaviors have on your connections with others?
3. How can you maintain and strengthen these practices in your relationships?

Day 309: Affirmation for Purpose

Affirmation: "I align my actions with my purpose by setting clear goals and taking deliberate steps towards achieving them."

Explanation: Setting clear goals and taking deliberate steps align your actions with your purpose. This affirmation supports purposeful and strategic efforts toward your objectives.

Reflection Questions:

1. What clear goals did you set, and what deliberate steps did you take towards them today?

2. How did these actions align with your purpose?
3. How can you refine your goal-setting and action plans to stay aligned with your purpose?

Day 310: Affirmation for Self-Confidence

Affirmation: "I empower myself by setting boundaries, prioritizing my needs, and valuing my self-worth."

Explanation: Setting boundaries, prioritizing your needs, and valuing your self-worth empower self-confidence. This affirmation promotes healthy self-regard and personal empowerment.

Reflection Questions:

1. How did you set boundaries, prioritize your needs, and value your self-worth today?
2. What impact did these actions have on your self-confidence?
3. How can you continue to empower yourself through these practices?

Day 311: Affirmation for Positivity

Affirmation: "I maintain a positive outlook by practicing gratitude and focusing on the good in every situation."

Explanation: Practicing gratitude and focusing on the good helps maintain a positive outlook. This affirmation supports a grateful and optimistic approach to life.

Reflection Questions:

1. What aspects of your life did you practice gratitude for today?
2. How did focusing on the good influence your outlook and mood?
3. How can you continue to cultivate gratitude and positivity in your daily life?

Day 312: Affirmation for Security

Affirmation: "I enhance my sense of security by fostering a stable environment and nurturing supportive relationships."

Explanation: Fostering a stable environment and nurturing supportive relationships enhance your sense of security. This affirmation supports a balanced and secure personal life.

Reflection Questions:

1. How did you create a stable environment and nurture supportive relationships today?
2. What effects did these actions have on your sense of

security?

3. How can you continue to develop stability and support in your life?

Day 313: Affirmation for Wealth

Affirmation: "I build wealth by making wise financial choices and staying disciplined in my spending and saving habits."

Explanation: Making wise financial choices and staying disciplined in spending and saving build wealth. This affirmation promotes responsible and strategic financial management.

Reflection Questions:

1. What wise financial choices did you make today, and how did they impact your wealth?
2. How did discipline in spending and saving contribute to your financial goals?
3. How can you improve your financial habits to enhance your wealth-building efforts?

Day 314: Affirmation for Love

Affirmation: "I cultivate loving relationships by being forgiving, patient, and expressing appreciation for those I care about."

Explanation: Forgiveness, patience, and expressing appreciation cultivate loving relationships. This affirmation encourages nurturing and supportive interactions with loved ones.

Reflection Questions:

1. How did you practice forgiveness, patience, and appreciation in your relationships today?
2. What effects did these practices have on your interactions with others?
3. How can you consistently integrate these qualities to deepen and enhance your relationships?

Day 315: Affirmation for Purpose

Affirmation: "I pursue my purpose with passion and resilience, embracing challenges as opportunities for growth."

Explanation: Pursuing your purpose with passion and resilience transforms challenges into opportunities for growth. This affirmation supports a determined and optimistic approach to fulfilling your goals.

Reflection Questions:

1. How did you approach challenges related to your purpose today?
2. What opportunities for growth did you identify in facing these challenges?
3. How can you continue to harness passion and resilience

in pursuing your purpose?

Day 316: Affirmation for Self-Confidence

Affirmation: "I bolster my self-confidence by celebrating my progress and acknowledging my capabilities."

Explanation: Celebrating your progress and acknowledging your capabilities reinforce self-confidence. This affirmation encourages self-recognition and positive reinforcement.

Reflection Questions:

1. What progress did you celebrate today, and how did it affect your confidence?
2. How did acknowledging your capabilities contribute to your self-esteem?
3. How can you maintain this practice to continuously build your self-confidence?

Day 317: Affirmation for Positivity

Affirmation: "I nurture positivity by surrounding myself with uplifting people and engaging in activities that bring me joy."

Explanation: Surrounding yourself with uplifting people and engaging in joyful activities fosters positivity. This affirmation promotes a supportive and fulfilling environment.

Reflection Questions:

1. Who were the uplifting people you interacted with today, and how did they impact your positivity?
2. What activities brought you joy, and how did they influence your mood?
3. How can you continue to create a positive and joyful environment in your life?

Day 318: Affirmation for Security

Affirmation: "I create a sense of security by establishing reliable routines and seeking stability in my daily life."

Explanation: Establishing reliable routines and seeking stability contribute to a sense of security. This affirmation encourages creating consistency and dependability in your daily life.

Reflection Questions:

1. What reliable routines did you establish today, and how did they affect your sense of security?
2. How did seeking stability influence your daily life?
3. What additional routines or practices can you implement to further enhance your security?

Day 319: Affirmation for Wealth

Affirmation: "I attract financial abundance by aligning my spending with my values and seeking opportunities to increase my wealth."

Explanation: Aligning spending with values and seeking opportunities for wealth increase attract financial abundance. This affirmation promotes ethical and proactive financial practices.

Reflection Questions:

1. How did aligning your spending with your values affect your financial situation today?
2. What opportunities did you explore to increase your wealth, and what were the results?
3. How can you continue to integrate your values and seek new opportunities to attract abundance?

Day 320: Affirmation for Love

Affirmation: "I strengthen my relationships by showing empathy, actively listening, and offering unwavering support."

Explanation: Showing empathy, actively listening, and offering unwavering support strengthen relationships. This affirmation promotes deep and meaningful connections with others.

Reflection Questions:

1. How did you demonstrate empathy, active listening, and support in your relationships today?
2. What effects did these actions have on your interactions and relationships?
3. How can you consistently apply these practices to nurture and strengthen your connections?

Day 321: Affirmation for Purpose

Affirmation: "I align my daily actions with my long-term goals, staying focused and committed to my purpose."

Explanation: Aligning daily actions with long-term goals fosters focus and commitment to your purpose. This affirmation supports a disciplined and purposeful approach to achieving your objectives.

Reflection Questions:

1. How did you align your daily actions with your long-term goals today?
2. What impact did this alignment have on your focus and commitment to your purpose?
3. How can you refine your daily actions to better support your long-term objectives?

Day 322: Affirmation for Self-Confidence

Affirmation: "I enhance my self-confidence by stepping out of my comfort zone and embracing new challenges."

Explanation: Stepping out of your comfort zone and embracing new challenges build self-confidence. This affirmation encourages personal growth and courage.

Reflection Questions:

1. What new challenges did you embrace today, and how did they affect your confidence?
2. How did stepping out of your comfort zone contribute to your personal growth?
3. How can you continue to seek and embrace challenges to further boost your self-confidence?

Day 323: Affirmation for Positivity

Affirmation: "I cultivate a positive mindset by practicing mindfulness and focusing on the present moment."

Explanation: Practicing mindfulness and focusing on the present moment cultivate a positive mindset. This affirmation supports mental clarity and emotional well-being.

Reflection Questions:

1. How did practicing mindfulness and focusing on the present moment impact your mindset today?
2. What benefits did you experience from being more

present and aware?

3. How can you incorporate mindfulness practices into your daily routine to maintain positivity?

Day 324: Affirmation for Security

Affirmation: "I foster a sense of security by building strong support networks and maintaining a balanced lifestyle."

Explanation: Building strong support networks and maintaining a balanced lifestyle foster a sense of security. This affirmation encourages creating a stable and supportive environment.

Reflection Questions:

1. How did you build or strengthen your support network today?
2. What steps did you take to maintain a balanced lifestyle, and how did they impact your security?
3. How can you continue to develop and maintain strong support systems and balance in your life?

Day 325: Affirmation for Wealth

Affirmation: "I achieve financial success by setting clear financial goals and taking consistent actions to reach them."

Explanation: Setting clear financial goals and taking consistent actions support financial success. This affirmation promotes strategic planning and dedication to financial growth.

Reflection Questions:

1. What financial goals did you set, and what consistent actions did you take towards achieving them today?
2. How did these actions impact your progress toward financial success?
3. How can you refine your goal-setting and actions to enhance your financial achievements?

Day 326: Affirmation for Love

Affirmation: "I nurture love in my life by expressing gratitude, being present, and sharing meaningful moments with those I cherish."

Explanation: Expressing gratitude, being present, and sharing meaningful moments nurture love. This affirmation supports the cultivation of deep and appreciative relationships.

Reflection Questions:

1. How did you express gratitude, be present, and share meaningful moments in your relationships today?

247

2. What effects did these actions have on your connections with others?
3. How can you continue to practice these behaviors to enhance and sustain love in your life?

Day 327: Affirmation for Purpose

Affirmation: "I pursue my purpose with determination and flexibility, adapting to change and staying committed to my vision."

Explanation: Determination and flexibility in pursuing your purpose support resilience and adaptability. This affirmation encourages staying committed while being open to change.

Reflection Questions:

1. How did you demonstrate determination and flexibility in pursuing your purpose today?
2. What changes or challenges did you encounter, and how did you adapt to them?
3. How can you maintain both determination and flexibility in your ongoing pursuit of your purpose?

Day 328: Affirmation for Self-Confidence

Affirmation: "I build my self-confidence by recognizing my growth, celebrating my successes, and affirming my worth."

Explanation: Recognizing growth, celebrating successes, and affirming your worth build self-confidence. This affirmation supports a positive and affirming view of yourself.

Reflection Questions:

1. What aspects of your growth did you recognize today, and how did this affect your confidence?
2. How did celebrating your successes contribute to your self-esteem?
3. How can you regularly affirm your worth to maintain and build your self-confidence?

Day 329: Affirmation for Positivity

Affirmation: "I foster a positive environment by surrounding myself with inspiring people and engaging in activities that uplift my spirit."

Explanation: Surrounding yourself with inspiring people and engaging in uplifting activities foster a positive environment. This affirmation supports a joyful and motivating atmosphere.

Reflection Questions:

1. Who were the inspiring people you interacted with today,

and how did they affect your positivity?

2. What uplifting activities did you engage in, and what impact did they have on your mood?
3. How can you continue to create and sustain a positive and inspiring environment?

Day 330: Affirmation for Security

Affirmation: "I enhance my security by creating a structured plan, managing my resources wisely, and staying prepared for unforeseen events."

Explanation: Creating a structured plan, managing resources wisely, and staying prepared enhance security. This affirmation supports strategic and proactive approaches to personal stability.

Reflection Questions:

1. What structured plans did you create, and how did you manage your resources wisely today?
2. How did these actions contribute to your sense of security?
3. What additional steps can you take to improve your preparation and stability for unforeseen events?

Day 331: Affirmation for Wealth

Affirmation: "I attract and manage wealth with integrity and wisdom, using my resources to create value and opportunities."

Explanation: Attracting and managing wealth with integrity and wisdom fosters sustainable financial growth. This affirmation emphasizes the importance of ethical practices and resourcefulness.

Reflection Questions:

1. How did you attract and manage wealth with integrity and wisdom today?
2. What value did you create with your resources, and what opportunities did you explore?
3. How can you continue to integrate integrity and wisdom into your financial practices?

Day 332: Affirmation for Love

Affirmation: "I deepen my love connections by showing appreciation, being emotionally available, and nurturing trust."

Explanation: Showing appreciation, being emotionally available, and nurturing trust strengthen love connections. This affirmation promotes a deeper and more meaningful relationship dynamic.

Reflection Questions:

1. How did you show appreciation and emotional availability in your relationships today?
2. What steps did you take to nurture trust, and what effects did this have?
3. How can you maintain and enhance these practices to deepen your love connections?

Day 333: Affirmation for Purpose

Affirmation: "I remain focused on my purpose by setting clear intentions, prioritizing my goals, and staying resilient in the face of obstacles."

Explanation: Setting clear intentions, prioritizing goals, and remaining resilient support a focused pursuit of your purpose. This affirmation reinforces determination and strategic planning.

Reflection Questions:

1. What clear intentions did you set for your purpose today, and how did you prioritize your goals?
2. How did you demonstrate resilience in the face of obstacles?
3. How can you enhance your focus and resilience in pursuing your purpose?

Day 334: Affirmation for Self-Confidence

Affirmation: "I cultivate self-confidence by acknowledging my strengths, embracing my uniqueness, and celebrating my achievements."

Explanation: Acknowledging strengths, embracing uniqueness, and celebrating achievements build self-confidence. This affirmation supports a positive self-image and recognition of personal accomplishments.

Reflection Questions:

1. How did you acknowledge your strengths and embrace your uniqueness today?
2. What achievements did you celebrate, and how did this affect your self-confidence?
3. How can you continue to recognize and celebrate your strengths and accomplishments?

Day 335: Affirmation for Positivity

Affirmation: "I maintain positivity by focusing on solutions, practicing gratitude, and surrounding myself with encouraging influences."

Explanation: Focusing on solutions, practicing gratitude, and surrounding yourself with encouraging influences sustain positivity. This affirmation promotes a proactive and grateful mindset.

Reflection Questions:

1. How did you focus on solutions and practice gratitude today?
2. What encouraging influences did you surround yourself with, and how did they impact your mood?
3. How can you maintain and enhance these practices to foster ongoing positivity?

Day 336: Affirmation for Security

Affirmation: "I strengthen my sense of security by building healthy habits, setting realistic goals, and creating a stable environment."

Explanation: Building healthy habits, setting realistic goals, and creating a stable environment reinforce a sense of security. This affirmation supports a balanced and structured approach to personal stability.

Reflection Questions:

1. What healthy habits did you build, and how did they contribute to your sense of security today?
2. How did setting realistic goals and creating a stable environment impact your stability?
3. What additional actions can you take to further enhance your sense of security?

Day 337: Affirmation for Wealth

Affirmation: "I cultivate wealth by investing in my growth, seeking knowledge, and making informed financial decisions."

Explanation: Investing in personal growth, seeking knowledge, and making informed decisions support wealth cultivation. This affirmation encourages continuous learning and strategic financial planning.

Reflection Questions:

1. How did you invest in your growth and seek knowledge today?
2. What informed financial decisions did you make, and what was their impact?
3. How can you continue to invest in your growth and knowledge to enhance your wealth?

Day 338: Affirmation for Love

Affirmation: "I enrich my relationships by being present, communicating openly, and showing unwavering support."

Explanation: Being present, communicating openly, and showing support enrich relationships. This affirmation promotes deeper and more fulfilling connections with others.

Reflection Questions:

1. How did you practice being present and communicating openly in your relationships today?

2. In what ways did you show unwavering support, and what effects did this have?

3. How can you continue to enrich your relationships through these practices?

Day 339: Affirmation for Purpose

Affirmation: "I advance my purpose by taking purposeful actions, learning from experiences, and adapting my approach as needed."

Explanation: Taking purposeful actions, learning from experiences, and adapting your approach drive progress toward your purpose. This affirmation supports a dynamic and evolving pursuit of your goals.

Reflection Questions:

1. What purposeful actions did you take today, and how did they advance your purpose?

2. What experiences did you learn from, and how did they influence your approach?

3. How can you continue to adapt and evolve in your pursuit of your purpose?

Day 340: Affirmation for Self-Confidence

Affirmation: "I enhance my self-confidence by setting achievable goals, acknowledging my progress, and embracing my potential."

Explanation: Setting achievable goals, acknowledging progress, and embracing potential strengthen self-confidence. This affirmation promotes a positive and proactive approach to personal growth.

Reflection Questions:

1. What achievable goals did you set, and how did you acknowledge your progress today?
2. How did embracing your potential contribute to your self-confidence?
3. How can you continue to set goals and recognize progress to build your confidence?

Day 341: Affirmation for Positivity

Affirmation: "I foster positivity by celebrating small victories, practicing self-compassion, and maintaining an optimistic outlook."

Explanation: Celebrating small victories, practicing self-compassion, and maintaining optimism support a positive mindset. This affirmation encourages appreciation of progress and kindness toward oneself.

Reflection Questions:

1. What small victories did you celebrate today, and how did they impact your positivity?
2. How did practicing self-compassion influence your outlook?
3. How can you continue to celebrate achievements and maintain an optimistic perspective?

Day 342: Affirmation for Security

Affirmation: "I build a solid foundation of security by managing my finances wisely, nurturing my well-being, and planning for the future."

Explanation: Managing finances wisely, nurturing well-being, and planning for the future create a solid foundation of security. This affirmation supports comprehensive and proactive approaches to stability.

Reflection Questions:

1. How did you manage your finances and nurture your well-being today?
2. What steps did you take to plan for the future, and how did they affect your sense of security?
3. How can you enhance your strategies for financial management, well-being, and future planning?

Day 343: Affirmation for Wealth

Affirmation: "I attract abundance by aligning my financial goals with my values and seeking opportunities for growth and investment."

Explanation: Aligning financial goals with values and seeking growth and investment opportunities attract abundance. This affirmation promotes ethical financial practices and proactive investment.

Reflection Questions:

1. How did you align your financial goals with your values today?
2. What opportunities for growth and investment did you pursue, and what were the outcomes?
3. How can you continue to integrate your values and seek opportunities to attract abundance?

Day 344: Affirmation for Love

Affirmation: "I deepen my connections by expressing my true self, practicing active listening, and valuing the unique qualities of others."

Explanation: Expressing your true self, practicing active listening, and valuing others' qualities deepen connections. This affirmation fosters authenticity and appreciation in relationships.

Reflection Questions:

1. How did you express your true self and practice active listening in your relationships today?
2. In what ways did you value the unique qualities of others, and what effects did this have?
3. How can you continue to deepen your connections through these practices?

Day 345: Affirmation for Purpose

Affirmation: "I drive my purpose forward by setting clear priorities, taking inspired action, and staying focused on my vision."

Explanation: Setting priorities, taking inspired action, and staying focused drive progress toward your purpose. This affirmation supports clarity and determination in pursuing your goals.

Reflection Questions:

1. What clear priorities did you set, and how did they guide your actions today?
2. How did taking inspired action and maintaining focus influence your progress?
3. How can you refine your priorities and actions to better support your purpose?

Day 346: Affirmation for Self-Confidence

Affirmation: "I build self-confidence by embracing my uniqueness, setting personal boundaries, and celebrating my growth."

Explanation: Embracing uniqueness, setting boundaries, and celebrating growth build self-confidence. This affirmation encourages self-acceptance and assertiveness.

Reflection Questions:

1. How did embracing your uniqueness and setting boundaries contribute to your self-confidence today?
2. What aspects of your growth did you celebrate, and how did this impact your self-esteem?
3. How can you continue to embrace your individuality and maintain healthy boundaries?

Day 347: Affirmation for Positivity

Affirmation: "I nurture positivity by focusing on what I can control, practicing gratitude, and spreading kindness."

Explanation: Focusing on what you can control, practicing gratitude, and spreading kindness nurture positivity. This affirmation supports a proactive and grateful approach to life.

Reflection Questions:

1. How did focusing on controllable aspects and practicing gratitude influence your positivity today?
2. In what ways did you spread kindness, and how did it

261

affect your outlook?

3. What additional steps can you take to enhance your sense of positivity?

Day 348: Affirmation for Security

Affirmation: "I enhance my security by making thoughtful decisions, fostering strong relationships, and staying prepared for challenges."

Explanation: Making thoughtful decisions, fostering strong relationships, and staying prepared enhance security. This affirmation emphasizes the importance of deliberate choices and support networks.

Reflection Questions:

1. How did thoughtful decision-making and fostering relationships contribute to your sense of security today?
2. What steps did you take to prepare for potential challenges, and how did they impact your feeling of stability?
3. How can you continue to build and maintain your sense of security through these practices?

Day 349: Affirmation for Wealth

Affirmation: "I attract financial success by staying informed, making strategic investments, and maintaining a positive mindset."

Explanation: Staying informed, making strategic investments, and maintaining positivity attract financial success. This affirmation promotes a balanced approach to wealth creation.

Reflection Questions:

1. What actions did you take to stay informed about financial matters today?
2. How did your strategic investments and positive mindset influence your financial progress?
3. What further steps can you take to enhance your financial success?

Day 350: Affirmation for Love

Affirmation: "I nurture love by being empathetic, practicing forgiveness, and appreciating the journey of growth with others."

Explanation: Being empathetic, practicing forgiveness, and appreciating growth in relationships nurture love. This affirmation supports a compassionate and understanding approach to relationships.

Reflection Questions:

1. How did empathy and forgiveness play a role in your interactions today?
2. What aspects of the journey with your loved ones did you appreciate, and how did it affect your relationships?
3. How can you further nurture love through empathy, forgiveness, and appreciation?

Day 351: Affirmation for Purpose

Affirmation: "I pursue my purpose with passion by setting inspiring goals, taking consistent actions, and reflecting on my progress."

Explanation: Setting inspiring goals, taking consistent actions, and reflecting on progress help in the passionate pursuit of purpose. This affirmation supports dedication and evaluation in goal achievement.

Reflection Questions:

1. What inspiring goals did you set today, and how did they motivate your actions?
2. How did your consistent actions contribute to your purpose, and what did you learn from reflecting on your progress?
3. How can you maintain and enhance your passionate pursuit of purpose?

Day 352: Affirmation for Self-Confidence

Affirmation: "I boost my self-confidence by challenging limiting beliefs, celebrating my successes, and affirming my worth."

Explanation: Challenging limiting beliefs, celebrating successes, and affirming worth boost self-confidence. This affirmation encourages overcoming self-doubt and recognizing personal achievements.

Reflection Questions:

1. What limiting beliefs did you challenge today, and how did this impact your self-confidence?
2. How did celebrating your successes influence your self-esteem?
3. How can you continue to affirm your worth and challenge self-limiting beliefs?

Day 353: Affirmation for Positivity

Affirmation: "I foster positivity by surrounding myself with supportive people, engaging in uplifting activities, and focusing on the good in every situation."

Explanation: Surrounding yourself with supportive individuals, engaging in uplifting activities, and focusing on the positives cultivate a positive mindset. This affirmation emphasizes the importance of environment and perspective.

Reflection Questions:

265

1. How did the support from others and engaging in uplifting activities contribute to your positivity today?
2. What positive aspects did you focus on in challenging situations?
3. How can you further create a supportive environment and engage in activities that uplift you?

Day 354: Affirmation for Security

Affirmation: "I build lasting security by creating a solid plan, managing risks effectively, and fostering stability in my daily life."

Explanation: Creating a plan, managing risks, and fostering daily stability build lasting security. This affirmation supports proactive planning and risk management.

Reflection Questions:

1. What solid plans did you create today, and how did they contribute to your security?
2. How did you manage risks effectively, and what impact did this have on your sense of stability?
3. What additional actions can you take to further enhance your security and stability?

Day 355: Affirmation for Wealth

Affirmation: "I achieve financial abundance by setting clear intentions, taking proactive steps, and continuously learning about wealth-building strategies."

Explanation: Setting intentions, taking proactive steps, and learning about wealth-building strategies lead to financial abundance. This affirmation emphasizes clarity, action, and ongoing education.

Reflection Questions:

1. What clear intentions did you set for your financial goals today?
2. How did your proactive steps and learning about wealth-building strategies contribute to your financial progress?
3. What further actions can you take to achieve and maintain financial abundance?

Day 356: Affirmation for Love

Affirmation: "I enrich my relationships by being present, expressing gratitude, and offering unconditional support."

Explanation: Being present, expressing gratitude, and offering support enrich relationships. This affirmation fosters deeper connections and mutual appreciation.

Reflection Questions:

1. How did being present and expressing gratitude enhance

your relationships today?

2. In what ways did you offer unconditional support, and how did it affect your connections?

3. How can you continue to enrich your relationships through presence, gratitude, and support?

Day 357: Affirmation for Purpose

Affirmation: "I align with my purpose by staying focused on my vision, embracing opportunities for growth, and reflecting on my achievements."

Explanation: Staying focused, embracing growth opportunities, and reflecting on achievements align you with your purpose. This affirmation supports a strategic and reflective approach to goal-setting.

Reflection Questions:

1. How did staying focused on your vision guide your actions today?

2. What opportunities for growth did you embrace, and how did they align with your purpose?

3. How can you enhance your alignment with your purpose through focus, growth, and reflection?

Day 358: Affirmation for Self-Confidence

Affirmation: "I strengthen my self-confidence by acknowledging my strengths, taking pride in my accomplishments, and embracing my potential."

Explanation: Acknowledging strengths, taking pride in accomplishments, and embracing potential strengthen self-confidence. This affirmation supports a positive self-view and recognition of capabilities.

Reflection Questions:

1. How did acknowledging your strengths and taking pride in accomplishments influence your self-confidence today?
2. In what ways did you embrace your potential, and how did it affect your self-esteem?
3. How can you continue to build and maintain your self-confidence through recognition and pride?

Day 359: Affirmation for Positivity

Affirmation: "I cultivate positivity by maintaining an optimistic attitude, practicing self-care, and celebrating the good in my life."

Explanation: Maintaining optimism, practicing self-care, and celebrating the good cultivate positivity. This affirmation supports a proactive and nurturing approach to a positive mindset.

Reflection Questions:

1. How did maintaining an optimistic attitude and practicing self-care contribute to your positivity today?
2. What aspects of your life did you celebrate, and how did this enhance your outlook?
3. How can you continue to nurture positivity through optimism, self-care, and celebration?

Day 360: Affirmation for Security

Affirmation: "I create a sense of security by managing my resources wisely, building supportive relationships, and staying adaptable to change."

Explanation: Managing resources wisely, building relationships, and staying adaptable create security. This affirmation emphasizes the importance of resource management, support networks, and flexibility.

Reflection Questions:

1. How did managing your resources wisely and building relationships contribute to your sense of security today?
2. What steps did you take to stay adaptable to change, and how did it impact your stability?
3. What further actions can you take to enhance your sense of security through resource management and adaptability?

Day 361: Affirmation for Purpose

Affirmation: "I am guided by my passions, and they lead me to my purpose."

Explanation: Passion often serves as a compass guiding you toward your purpose. This affirmation encourages you to follow your passions, trusting that they will lead you to a fulfilling and meaningful life.

Reflection Questions:

1. What are you most passionate about in life?
2. How can you incorporate your passions into your daily routine?
3. In what ways have your passions guided your decisions and actions today?

Day 362: Affirmation for Success

Affirmation: "I trust in my abilities to succeed in all that I do."

Explanation: Belief in your abilities is crucial for success. This affirmation helps to reinforce self-confidence, reminding you that you have the skills and strengths necessary to achieve your goals.

Reflection Questions:

1. What abilities or strengths did you rely on today to overcome challenges?
2. How can you build confidence in areas where you feel less

capable?

3. What successes have you achieved that demonstrate your abilities?

Day 363: Affirmation for Happiness

Affirmation: "I surround myself with people who uplift and inspire me."

Explanation: The people around you greatly influence your happiness. This affirmation encourages you to build a supportive and positive community, recognizing the impact that uplifting relationships can have on your well-being.

Reflection Questions:

1. Who in your life uplifts and inspires you the most?
2. How can you nurture and strengthen these relationships?
3. How did your interactions with others impact your happiness today?

Day 364: Affirmation for Purpose

Affirmation: "I am living my purpose each day with intention and passion."

Explanation: Purpose is not just about the future; it's about how you live each day. This affirmation encourages you to approach every day with intention, aligning your actions with your purpose and passion.

Reflection Questions:

1. How did you live with purpose and intention today?
2. What actions today felt most aligned with your passion?
3. How can you ensure that your daily actions reflect your purpose?

Day 365: Affirmation for Success

Affirmation: "I take action toward my goals every day, no matter how small the step."

Explanation: Success is often built on small, consistent actions. This affirmation is a reminder that progress, no matter how small, is valuable and brings you closer to your goals. It encourages daily effort and perseverance.

Reflection Questions:

1. What small actions did you take today to move toward your goals?
2. How can you maintain momentum even when progress feels slow?
3. What strategies can you implement to ensure you take daily steps toward success?

These affirmations and reflections are tools to help you cultivate a positive mindset. They are not a magic formula for instant happiness, purpose, and success. Consistent effort and belief in yourself are essential for achieving your goals.

10

Conclusion

Positive affirmations are more than just a collection of up-lifting phrases—they are a powerful tool for personal trans-formation and growth. They offer a straightforward yet remarkably effective method for shifting your mindset, im-proving mental health, and achieving your goals. Find yourself facing challenges, aiming to enhance your relationships, or simply wishing to cultivate a more positive outlook on life. Affirmations can be a valuable ally in providing the support and encouragement you need.

At their core, positive affirmations are deliberate, positive statements that you repeat to yourself to influence your thoughts and emotions. They work by embedding these positive beliefs into your subconscious mind, gradually reshaping your attitudes and behaviors. Regularly affirming these positive statements creates a mental environment that supports your goals and fosters a more optimistic perspective.

Understanding the science behind affirmations can significantly enhance their effectiveness. Research into cognitive psychology and neuroplasticity reveals that our thoughts profoundly impact our mental and emotional states. Affirmations leverage this principle by reinforcing positive thought patterns and helping to rewire the brain. When you repeatedly affirm positive statements, you strengthen the neural pathways associated with those thoughts, making them more likely to influence your behavior and outlook. This process is akin to training your brain to adopt a more positive and constructive mindset.

One key to successfully incorporating affirmations into your life is consistency. Consistent practice is essential for affirmations to take root and yield tangible results. Just as physical exercise requires regularity to achieve fitness goals, affirmations need to be practiced consistently to effect change. Establish a routine that integrates affirmations into your daily life. For instance, you might start your day with a few minutes of affirmations during your morning routine or end your day by reflecting on your affirmations before bed. The more frequently you engage with these positive statements, the more deeply they will be ingrained in your subconscious.

Belief is another crucial component in the effectiveness of affirmations. Simply reciting positive statements without genuine belief in their truth will not yield the desired results. To truly benefit from affirmations, you need to foster a deep sense of conviction in the statements you are affirming. This involves more than just saying the words—it requires internalizing them and allowing them to resonate with your core values and aspirations. If you struggle with belief in your affirmations, start by choosing statements that feel achievable and relevant to your current situation. As you begin to experience small successes, your belief in the affirmations will grow, reinforcing their impact.

In addition to addressing specific challenges or goals, affirmations can also enhance relationships and overall well-being. For example, affirmations focused on self-love and acceptance, such as "I am worthy of love and respect" or "I honor and accept myself just as I am," can help build a healthier relationship with yourself. This self-acceptance, in turn, positively influences your interactions with others, fostering more meaningful and supportive connections.

Similarly, affirmations can be a valuable tool for overcoming obstacles and developing resilience. Statements like "I am capable of handling any challenge" or "I grow stronger with each experience" can help you navigate difficult situations with a more positive and proactive attitude. By reinforcing a mindset of resilience and strength, affirmations support your ability to bounce back from adversity and maintain a forward-looking perspective.

To maximize the benefits of affirmations, consider incorporating them into various aspects of your life. For instance, you might use a journal to write down your affirmations and reflections, creating a tangible record of your progress. This practice not only helps you stay organized but also deepens your engagement with the positive changes you're striving for. Additionally, using visual reminders, such as affirmation cards or sticky notes placed in prominent locations, can keep your affirmations at the forefront of your mind throughout the day.

Another effective strategy is to pair affirmations with other positive habits. For example, you might integrate affirmations into your morning routine by reciting them while you prepare for the day or combine them with relaxation techniques such as meditation or deep breathing exercises. By aligning affirmations with established routines, you create a seamless practice that enhances their effectiveness and reinforces their impact on your daily life.

As you embark on your affirmation journey, remember that patience and perseverance are essential. The transformation process through affirmations is gradual, and it may take time to see significant changes. However, with consistent practice and a steadfast belief in the affirmations you are using, you will begin to notice positive shifts in your mindset, behavior, and overall well-being.

Positive affirmations can unlock your full potential and lead you toward a more fulfilling and happier life. By understanding the science behind them, applying them consistently, and maintaining a strong belief in their effectiveness, you can harness the power of affirmations to create the life you desire. Embrace this transformative tool with dedication, and watch as it helps you achieve your goals and foster a more positive and empowered outlook on life.

* * *

Now you have everything you need to practice your positive affirmations daily; it's time to pass on your newfound knowledge and show other readers where they can find the same help.

Simply by leaving your honest review of this book, you'll show others where they can find the positive transformation they're looking for and pass their passion for positivity forward.

11

Tracking Your Affirmation Habit

Tracking your positive affirmation practice is a powerful way to reinforce the behavior and help turn it into a daily habit. By keeping a record of your affirmations, you're not only committing to the practice but also holding yourself accountable. Writing down your affirmations or using a habit tracker can serve as a visual reminder, prompting consistency and helping you stay focused. Over time, as you see your progress in real-time, it encourages you to keep going, and the positive changes become more noticeable.

Reinforcing positive affirmations daily creates a feedback loop where repeating these affirmations shapes your mindset. As you continue to track, you'll notice patterns in your mood and behavior, confirming that the practice influences how you think and feel. This can serve as additional motivation. When you track your progress, you can also reflect on any challenges, helping you refine the affirmations to fit your goals better, strengthening the practice even more.

Tracking your affirmation habit can also help solidify it in your routine by giving you tangible evidence of its benefits. You can mark the days when you've completed your practice and note any positive outcomes, which builds a sense of accomplishment. As with any habit, repetition is key, and by tracking your affirmations, you're more likely to integrate them into your daily life naturally, allowing the positive mindset they foster to become part of your default thought patterns.

Use this Affirmation Tracker to help you track and help reinforce your new habit throughout the year.

AFFIRMATION TRACKER

JAN	FEB	MAR	APR	MAY	JUN	JUL	AUG	SEP	OCT	NOV	DES
1	1	1	1	1	1	1	1	1	1	1	1
2	2	2	2	2	2	2	2	2	2	2	2
3	3	3	3	3	3	3	3	3	3	3	3
4	4	4	4	4	4	4	4	4	4	4	4
5	5	5	5	5	5	5	5	5	5	5	5
6	6	6	6	6	6	6	6	6	6	6	6
7	7	7	7	7	7	7	7	7	7	7	7
8	8	8	8	8	8	8	8	8	8	8	8
9	9	9	9	9	9	9	9	9	9	9	9
10	10	10	10	10	10	10	10	10	10	10	10
11	11	11	11	11	11	11	11	11	11	11	11
12	12	12	12	12	12	12	12	12	12	12	12
13	13	13	13	13	13	13	13	13	13	13	13
14	14	14	14	14	14	14	14	14	14	14	14
15	15	15	15	15	15	15	15	15	15	15	15
16	16	16	16	16	16	16	16	16	16	16	16
17	17	17	17	17	17	17	17	17	17	17	17
18	18	18	18	18	18	18	18	18	18	18	18
19	19	19	19	19	19	19	19	19	19	19	19
20	20	20	20	20	20	20	20	20	20	20	20
21	21	21	21	21	21	21	21	21	21	21	21
22	22	22	22	22	22	22	22	22	22	22	22
23	23	23	23	23	23	23	23	23	23	23	23
24	24	24	24	24	24	24	24	24	24	24	24
25	25	25	25	25	25	25	25	25	25	25	25
26	26	26	26	26	26	26	26	26	26	26	26
27	27	27	27	27	27	27	27	27	27	27	27
28	28	28	28	28	28	28	28	28	28	28	28
29	29	29	29	29	29	29	29	29	29	29	29
30	30	30	30	30	30	30	30	30	30	30	30
31	31	31	31	31	31	31	31	31	31	31	31

12

BONUS AFFIRMATIONS AND MEDITATIONS

If you're as enthusiastic about affirmations as I am, you're probably always looking for new and fun ways to sprinkle positivity into your everyday routine!

To keep your affirmation game strong and exciting,, I've crafted a specially curated YouTube playlist filled with a delightful mix of uplifting daily affirmations. Whether you're looking for quick bursts of inspiration or longer, immersive sessions, this playlist has something to seamlessly fit into your busy day.

Ready to dive into a world of positivity? Scan the code below to explore this collection and take your affirmation game to the next level! ☆📖

* * *

Meditation and positive affirmations are a powerful combination for nurturing inner peace and cultivating a positive mindset. When used together, they create a harmonious practice that calms the mind and reinforces positive beliefs and intentions. Meditation helps quiet the mental chatter, allowing you to connect more deeply with the affirmations you repeat.

This synergy enhances focus, reduces stress, and promotes a deeper sense of well-being. To support your journey of inner transformation, I am also sharing a special playlist of Calm Guided Meditations by Rising Higher Meditation. These guided sessions will complement your affirmation practice, helping you achieve a serene and balanced state of mind.

Discover the benefits of this powerful duo by exploring the playlist through the link below.

About the Author

Amanda Otis is a passionate photographer, creative visionary, and dedicated coach. She crafts engaging ebooks, practical notebooks, and innovative digital products focusing on photography, organization, business, and generating passive income.

As a busy mom of nine, she thrives on outdoor adventures, traveling, hiking, and embracing new experiences with her family. Her love for continuous learning fuels her creative endeavors and personal growth.

You can connect with me on:

🌐 https://www.otispublishing.com

🐦 https://x.com/OtisPublising

📘 https://www.facebook.com/profile.php?id=61550110195806

🔗 https://linktr.ee/otis.publishing

🔗 https://amzn.to/41jjt37

Subscribe to my newsletter:

✉ https://www.honeybook.com/widget/otis_publishing_269430/cf_id/65a148f835369b002ceab84f

Also by Amanda Otis

The Grateful Heart: A Gratitude and Giving Journal with Positive Affirmations and Habit Tracking Pages

Discover the transformative power of gratitude and giving with this Gratitude and Giving Journal. This beautifully designed journal offers a comprehensive approach to cultivating a positive mindset and fostering daily reflection. Each page is thoughtfully crafted to guide you through daily and monthly gratitude practices, empowering affirmations, and insightful tracking sections.

Begin each day with a fresh perspective by recording your positive affirmations, setting the tone for a day filled with positivity and self-awareness. Use the daily tracking pages to note down the highlights, acts of kindness, and moments of gratitude, helping you to stay mindful and appreciative of life's blessings.

The monthly tracking sections provide an overview of your journey, allowing you to reflect on your progress, set new intentions, and celebrate your growth. Whether you're looking to improve your mental well-being, cultivate a habit of gratitude, or simply find more joy in everyday moments, this journal is your perfect companion.

Embrace the journey of gratitude and giving, and watch as it transforms your life one page at a time.

Eternal Ties: Our Family Heirloom Journal of History, Recipes, and Traditions

Dive into the heart of your family's history with our beautiful heirloom journal, "Eternal Ties." This book is more than just a collection of pages; it's a treasure trove of memories, family tree and genealogy charts, beloved heirloom recipes, cherished traditions, and important dates. Whether you're welcoming a new family member through marriage or celebrating an older child's graduation and independence, this journal makes the perfect heartfelt gift.

Key Features:

Family Tree & Genealogy: Trace your roots and document your lineage.

Heirloom Recipes: Preserve and pass down family culinary traditions.

Traditions & Memories: Capture the essence of your family's unique stories.

Important Dates: Never forget birthdays, anniversaries, and milestones.

Family Contact Information: Keep everyone connected and informed.

This journal is designed to be a keepsake that can be handed down through generations, ensuring your family's legacy lives on. Perfect for wedding gifts, graduation presents, or as a thoughtful gesture for any occasion!

Generations Gathered: A Family Legacy from Roots to Recipes, Heirloom Journal and Planner for Family Genealogy, Recipes, Traditions and Memories

Discover the treasures of your family's past and the flavors that have shaped generations in this heartfelt guidebook, perfect as a welcoming wedding gift or a cherished family keepsake for new adults embarking on their own journeys.

Inside these pages, you'll uncover a rich tapestry of history and tradition, blending family tree insights, cherished heirloom recipes, essential contact information, and a calendar of extended family birthdays and anniversaries. This book is not just a collection of facts; it's a celebration of the ties that bind us together.

Stay connected with your loved ones near and far with a comprehensive family contact section, ensuring you're always just a call or message away from those who matter most. Never miss an important date again with a specially curated calendar highlighting the birthdays and anniversaries of your extended family members.

Embark on a journey of discovery, connection, and celebration — your passport to the past, present, and future of your family's story.

Botanical Bliss: Your Complete Garden Planning Journal, Green Floral Plant, Garden, and Landscape Planner

Discover the art of gardening and unleash your green thumb with "Botanical Bliss," a comprehensive garden planning journal designed for enthusiasts of all levels. This beautifully crafted journal is your essential companion in creating and nurturing vibrant gardens that thrive with life and beauty.

Key Features:

Plant Inventory: Keep track of every plant in your garden, from perennials to vegetables, noting their varieties, locations, and care requirements.

Plant Diary: Chronicle the journey of each plant with detailed entries on growth progress, observations, pest control measures, and successes.

Harvest Log: Record bountiful harvests with dates, quantities, and notes on crop quality, inspiring future planting decisions and culinary adventures.

Garden Tips: Benefit from expert tips and practical advice on soil health, companion planting, pest management, and sustainable gardening practices.

Plant Information: Access comprehensive information on a wide range of plants, including sun and soil preferences, watering needs, and ideal companions for thriving gardens.

Garden Inspiration: Find inspiration in stunning garden photography, quotes from renowned gardeners, and creative ideas for garden layouts and designs.

Planting, Watering, and Scheduling Pages: Plan your garden with precision using graphed planning pages, watering schedules tailored to plant needs, and seasonal planting guides.

Graphed Planning Pages: Design your dream garden with customizable graphed pages for layouts, pathways, and structural elements like trellises and raised beds.

Garden Budget: Manage your garden finances effectively with budgeting tools, expense trackers, and cost-saving tips for a flourishing garden without breaking the bank.

"Botanical Bliss" empowers you to create harmonious and thriving gardens that reflect your passion for nature and beauty. Whether you're a seasoned gardener or just starting, this journal is your gateway to a world of botanical wonders and endless possibilities. Get ready to transform your garden into a vibrant oasis of color, fragrance, and joy!

www.ingramcontent.com/pod-product-compliance
Lightning Source LLC
Chambersburg PA
CBHW070910120626
46546CB00001B/202